Chai-ME

My Exploration of
Race, Religion, and
Spirituality in America

BY TAMAR MANASSEH

We have come over a way
that with tears has been watered.
We have come, treading our path
thro' the blood of the slaughtered,
Out from a gloomy past, till now we stand at last
Where the white gleam
of our bright star is cast.

–James Weldon Johnson

I would like to dedicate this book to the rabbis whose blood, sweat and tears have long watered the path on which I tread. May the memory of each of them forever be a blessing.

I would like to thank everyone from my past, my present and my future. This project wouldn't have been possible without you. I love all y'all!

TABLE OF CONTENTS

Introduction

Why would someone want to read a book about a black Jew? The answer is I don't know. However, I do know that week after week my synagogue is inundated with curious visitors who come for the experience, or maybe even to see if our blackness will somehow outweigh our Jewishness. After years of questions regarding my ethnicity, religion, and spirituality I figured it could best be explained in print form. From my earliest recollection I have been three things: black, female, and Jewish. I didn't come about those qualities separately and I never learned to see myself being one more than the others. I grew up with my mother, sister and nearly all of my cousins, aunts and uncles in a house headed by my grandmother. Most of the people in my family weren't Jewish. However, just as their secular and Christian traditions influenced us, our Judaism influenced them. I can remember playing dreidel with my cousins by the light of the Christmas tree and dressing up in my new clothes and eating matzah on Easter. My family had a respect for who I was and I for who they were. Unfortunately, this same respect was not extended to the world beyond our threshold.

Growing up a black Jew in the heart of a South Side Chicago ghetto was not a walk in the park. There was religion there, but not my kind. It was a rough neighborhood, plagued with violence. Some believed that they only survived there because of Jesus' grace and their involvement in the church, while others believed that their occasional mention of Jesus or the tattooed epitaphs displayed across their torso, arms, or back was their saving grace. I was not either of these people and it was sharply criticized whenever our differences were pointed out. To them a "Christ killer" or "confused," but I never felt like any of that. I grew up experiencing prejudice from a people who had learned to discriminate because they had been so discriminated against.

I also experienced prejudice from the people I identified religiously with. They would ask questions like, "Isn't being black and a woman already hard enough? Why would you *want* to be a Jew?" For the people who asked me this to assume that being a Jew was something that I *wanted* to be was like me assuming that their being Jews was something that they wanted to be.

Just as some black people didn't understand who I was, neither did most of my fellow Jews. I too lived in the same poverty that my neighbors did. I can remember eating government cheese and what food stamps looked like. I loved Malcolm X and Dr. Martin Luther King as much as other black people did, but I didn't embrace the religion of either of them. To many black folks, that meant I didn't embrace them or my true self. Just as Jews of European descent feel that their Judaism is decided by their parentage and God making them that way, so did I. Just as I didn't choose to be black or female, I didn't choose to be a Jew either. These decisions were made for me the exact same way that they were made for every other Jew. However, I am not often afforded the same understanding because I am black.

I am black and this has never been something that I ran from, nor have I ever wanted to be anything other than a woman, yet my religion has been something that I have struggled with quite a few times. It began when I was a child and I couldn't eat the hot dogs at a neighborhood barbecue and again when people made fun of me for being Jewish or going to a school that had a funny-sounding Hebrew name. There were other challenges too. I struggled with the demands of my faith the time Yom Kippur came on the same day as my high school homecoming dance, or the time I really wanted to get that mermaid tattoo. I struggled with how much my faith meant to me when a man I really liked would only propose if I converted to his religion. I struggled with it and questioned it, but I always came out the same way I went in: a Jew.

I have heard the personal accounts of European Jews who suffered isolation and anti-Semitism and I am certain at those times they too questioned their religion, but the same way I could not escape my Judaism, neither could they. This is not an account of the life and trials of every black Jew; it is my own story. My struggle to define my individual blackness and Jewishness is an echo of the struggle of every black person and every Jew: the struggle to be seen first as an individual, and not a member of a minority. I hope that my story will help my fellow Jews embrace what I feel is the highest Jewish ideal, "*Kol Yisrael arevim zeh la zeh*": All Israel is responsible for each other. This statement excludes race, ethnicity, or sect. It speaks to all Jews, wherever we are, at all times.

CHAPTER 1

IN THE BEGINNING   בְּרֵאשִׁית

On the morning of Friday, April 11, 2008, I had a moment. Well, maybe a little longer than a moment, for in that time that it seemed as if every hope, fear, joy, tragedy, and triumph of every ancestor who contributed to my existence all came together in a great and blinding light, a light so bright that it might shine back on a history not written by pens, and so far into a future full of possibilities so vast that a pen may not be capable of writing them all. But I decided to take my pen and write my part. That much I can do.

Friday, April 11, 2008 was the day before my daughter's Baht Mitzvah. I stood in the mirror curling my hair and I caught a glimpse of something in my face. It was only there for a moment, and I'm not even sure what it was, but it was something that made me think. I don't know if it was the way my bangs swept across my forehead and reminded me of my aunt Joyce, or if it was the way my hands looked as they gripped my Marcels, long piano fingers on a hand with prominent veins that lay beneath coco brown skin adorned with long oval fingernails, a constant reminder of my grandmother. As I stood there looking into my features, it seemed that I was looking at not just one face, but all of the faces. Ancestors known and unknown to me were there with me, in me, staring at each other. I stood there not seeing the faces of the children in my family, but the adults and the elders, and I realized even as I stood there living and breathing I was becoming a part of our history,

1

and the legacy which had been given me would one day be a part of a legacy that I would leave for someone else. I was black and comely, and I stood there and stared into the face of this woman, this woman who was a mother and who had a daughter that would be old enough to be a Baht Mitzvah the very next day, and I began to wonder, how did I get here?

Still staring at myself, I noticed the roundness of my face and the position of my cheekbones and the slant of my eyes and I thought of the little Ethiopian girl. A little Ethiopian girl was what my uncle David likened me to when I was a little girl. My mother told me the first time he ever saw me, he told her, "she looks like an Ethiopian." He never stopped saying that, and he would later lead my mother to a Temple with "Ethiopian" in its name. In the mirror, I saw the Ethiopian girl that my uncle David loved so much. I like to believe that he purposely gave me an African identity so I would never be confused about or unhappy with who I was, and he made sure I never was. Having him for an uncle was no mistake, I am certain. He was David and I was Tamar and he always treated me more like a daughter than a niece. He shared everything with me. He never took for granted what I could and couldn't understand, and he treated me like there wasn't anything that was too heavy for me to understand. He had the ability to explain things in a way that I could always comprehend. He wasn't like other adults, or other anyone, for that matter. Life had set before him a challenge that most others wouldn't have survived.

As a young man of only nineteen, my uncle was shot in his shoulder. This happened in 1963 in Chicago, and at that time Chicago had just as much racial hatred for Black people in the city as any small town, in any state in the south. He was a young black man, and an ambulance was a luxury that he wasn't afforded. The police tossed him in the back of the paddy wagon on the floor and that was that. En route to the hospital in the poorly-sprung van, the rough ride caused the bullet to migrate from his shoulder to his spinal cord and lodge there, ending any hope of him ever walking again. His legs would be amputated soon thereafter.

He spent many years after that in rehabilitative facilities and he would recount to me much later how difficult it was for him to deal with his paralysis. He was tall and handsome and he danced so well that he had earned the nickname "crazy legs," but that wasn't who he was anymore. The things that once defined him were gone, and now he was left with a new reality, in a new body, a lesser body, and he was clueless as to what to do with it. He would tell me how he went through a period when he wanted to die because he thought this new life didn't serve any purpose to anyone. But my uncle David had a higher purpose that wouldn't be revealed until many years later.

He told me a story about one day lying in the hospital bed of a Jewish hospital in Chicago and a Rabbi coming in to speak with him and see how he was doing. He told the Rabbi in jest that if he could show him a black Rabbi then he would become a Jew. The rabbi laughed and said, "I'll see you tomorrow, David." Believing that he had trumped the rabbi, Uncle David was surprised when the next day the rabbi came back with a black rabbi in tow. He told me that the first thing that this rabbi said to him was, "You know David is a Hebrew name, Right?" That was the beginning of what would be the journey of my life, even though I wouldn't be born for another decade. My uncle came home finally, but he was different. He had laid his old mind down and people just didn't treat him like they used to.

My uncle became totally dedicated to learning. It gave his life purpose. He would read and study all night long and most of the day. Where he once worried about where his legs couldn't take him, he now travelled the world and back, into the past and into the future through the power of his mind. He was no longer consumed by his paralysis; he had defeated it with his knowledge. His legs didn't make him; his brain did, and having learned he couldn't rely on just his physical attributes, he taught me that I couldn't either. I never knew him with legs. They had been amputated many years before I was born, but no one who had two legs and two arms ever had as much of an impact on me as my uncle did.

He was the first person in our family to revert back to Judaism, and even in a family that was never all that religious, he was still challenged and criticized. What others thought of him made no difference to him, another thing I learned from him. David spent nearly all of his time in study, so he knew and understood exactly who he was and why, and he was never afraid to explain the reasons for his change, although it was never much of an argument.

The problems came when he wouldn't eat my grandmother's ham or chitterlings, when he traded in the white port for Manishewitz, or wore his funny little cap. But the worse thing of all he didn't believe in Jesus anymore. The horror! Everyone was upset, but why? My family was never very religious in the first place. The only time I can ever remember going to church was for funerals, and under those circumstances, it doesn't really count. It wasn't about this new "religion" at all. It was about the old ideas and his rejection of them. It was because those recipes were passed down from generation to generation. My grandmother's oyster dressing recipe wasn't hers; it was her grandmother's and her great aunt's and so on. It wasn't about him praying on Saturday and lighting candles on Friday evening. It was about him doing something that he had not been taught by either of my grandparents to do. It wasn't even about Jesus or his role as the savior of mankind. It was about tradition and routine. No longer were the old traditions and routines good enough for him. If they were good enough for his parents and their parents and their parents, parents, then, who was he to reject them?

Growing up, David learned that Jesus was the guy in the picture, with eyes blue as the sea of Galilee, long flowing golden hair with skin as white as snow and later he told me, "Jesus must've never known my visiting hours". And it wasn't Jesus who visited him in the hospital. David had found new answers and a new purpose, which he was more than happy to share with any who would ask. He was a warrior. He was never afraid of a conversation or an argument, no matter how spirited it became, the fact that he was Black or that it wasn't tradition simply wasn't a good enough argument against him being an Israelite. He learned so much that after a while people hated to talk to him because his logical and compelling arguments could make even devout Christians question their own faith.

Even though he was in the minority, he became the guy that would say, yes, this is what I am, and why aren't you? He could quote Old Testament scripture, New Testament scripture, and the writings of Josephus, Maimonides, J.A. Rogers and other scholars and historians. It was his profound knowledge of who he was that helped him understand who everyone else was, and why, and even how. It was also this certainty of himself that would lead others to better know themselves, like my mother and even my grandmother.

My grandparents' story was like the stories that so many Black families during the great migration experienced. My grandparents, like most new arrivals to the North, struggled with poverty, hardship, and finding a new sense of community. My grandparents were different, though. They were always different and it is this difference that I believe brought my family to the point that gave my uncle the courage to question.

My family had a love/ hate relationship with religion. There were some who adopted their new-found religion lock, stock, and barrel and there were others who would not conform. Some were slaves in Mississippi and some in Alabama. There is a story in my family that one of my ancestors was the son of the governor of Alabama at that time. The governor wasn't married, had no children and was actually a unionist. He opposed secession and at one point left Alabama, going north to wait out the war. All of these factors would've made it even more difficult to admit to fathering a Black child. Tradition and census records verify that it was about this time when one of my great grand-mothers arrived in Mississippi with her son, David. I was always told he had a bitter hatred for white people and their religion. Perhaps it was because he and his mother had been rejected by his father. I suppose many Black people felt that way. He would grow up to marry a girl with extreme religious depth. Her family had been in Mississippi longer than her husband's. They had many children, some who shared their mother's faith, and others who became bootleggers and gamblers in Memphis. As she and her husband grew older, we find him in Memphis with some of their children and we find her in Alabama and later in Detroit with others. I believe that they loved each other, but they disagreed about the role and importance of religion in their lives and this is what caused them to separate. They never divorced or took up with anyone else.

My Grandfather would spend his early childhood with his religious grandmother, but the threat of beatings and lynching set him on the road. He landed in Memphis with his father and uncles. There he learned more about gambling, girls, and guns than he would about God. Both of my grandparents had difficult childhoods and were often displaced, and this instability kept them from developing a strong relationship with religion, but not from developing an ironclad one with God.

When my grandmother began having children, she became Catholic, not because she was raised that way, but because when she arrived in Chicago nearly destitute, the Catholic Church gave her the aid she so badly needed. She thought having a strong religious foundation was important for children, but she was never devout. Her faith in God and life experiences allowed her to raise children that were not afraid to look outside their church when they felt that their spiritual needs weren't being met by their religion. While she never had a church "home," God was her constant companion. In her lowest moments, she did nothing but question him, and he never turned away from her. After my uncle became a Jew, my mother would soon follow, and my Grandmother accepted their choice.

As was common for Black families then, I grew up in a house with nearly my entire family. My grandmother was the head of the family because my grandfather had died before I was born. I was the youngest of the many children in the house and I was constantly watched over. Daycare was a bad word in my house. When my mother went to work, there were always enough people at home to care for me. The rearing of the children in my family was far too important of a job to be outsourced. I had plenty of aunts, uncles and older cousins who took turns watching me. However, the majority of my time was spent with either my grandmother, who we all called Mama, or with my Uncle David and his wife Louise. During the day, I did everything with my grandmother. She wasn't as much fun as my uncle, but then again, who was?

The time I spent with my grandmother had a greater purpose than fun. It was during the trips to the light company to pay the bill, to the store on the alley to play her lottery numbers, and even over nightly games of solitaire that she would tell me the stories. The stories that would help me navigate through a world that she wouldn't always be around to help me through. The stories that gave me insight into her and her life and in turn would provide greater insight into my own.

My grandmother liked to talk about the old ways. The old ways were the way that her mother's family, religious North Carolinians, would do things. She wasn't a stranger to the Sabbath or to wearing a dress to go to pray, or covering her head as a sign of reverence. However, her mother and her mother's family did many things to my grandmother as a child that just didn't seem like things that good religious folk would do to a child, and perhaps this was why she elected to become Catholic. At some point my grandmother had shunned her mother's religion and her mother's mothers and so on. It was better for Black people in those days to say that they believed in Jesus than to say they weren't religious at all and be called a heathen.

Mama supported my uncle and all of us in her house who were Israelites in everything we did. It impressed her that I was learning to speak Hebrew and learning all about my culture. She thought it was really great that I knew things the grandchildren of her friends didn't. Her pride in me made me proud of myself. Where my other family members had once criticized my mother and uncle for their rediscovered identities, now they were far more understanding, if not accepting. They would give my sister and I gifts during Hanukkah, and my cousins loved to help celebrate that. What kid doesn't love gifts for eight days straight and playing dreidel and eating gelt and lighting a candle every day? And who could resist a potato latke? Hanukkah was never far from Christmas, and even though my family wasn't religious they still had a tree every year. It was pretty and it smelled good and it always sat atop a mountain of gifts. My grandmother always bought us new pajamas for Christmas Eve, and that was my favorite part. Christmas wasn't my holiday, but I learned I couldn't ruin it for everyone else by telling them it was fake and condemning them for their beliefs. I had to learn to be accepting of them the way that they had with me. I could play with their toys and even drink their eggnog and it wouldn't make me any more of a Christian than it made them Hebrews when they were playing dreidel with me. I had to keep in mind that there were more people like them than there was like me and I had to learn to respect that.

I looked forward to holidays and family times. My grandmother began modifying her recipes to be more conscious of everyone's dietary needs. For the Israelites in the house, it was kosher; for everyone else, it was just healthier. Instead of salt pork in her greens, Mama used smoked turkey. Instead of catfish with the spaghetti on Friday night, we'd have whitefish or buffalo and no one complained. Lox and gefilte may be the preferred fish of some Jews, but not where I came from. Easter always came around the same time as Pesach (Passover), which was torture for me. Imagine greens, baked macaroni and cheese, dressing, and cornbread and you can't eat any of it because it's Passover. There were always traces of religion in my house and in my neighborhood, but no one ever really went to church. There were Christmas trees, but no mass. There were Easter baskets and new suits and dresses, but still no mass. There were even cousins who went to Catholic school, but still no mass. I was growing up a Jew in the heart of what would become one of the worst ghettos in America. I had "religious" relatives and friends, in a neighborhood where the closest I got to anything that looked remotely Jewish were the six pointed stars with pitchforks coming from the top spray painted on every boarded up abandoned building I passed because it was the symbol of the street gang that occupied most of my neighborhood.

I knew early on that I was different, but I was okay with it. Around my friends I didn't much talk about being a Jew, since the subject was always met with laughter or disbelief. It would take me years to realize that they weren't being mean or nasty; they just didn't understand. As I got older, I began to envy them, though. They had it good. They didn't have to go to church, they could eat whatever they wanted, they could hang out all night on Friday and they still got gifts under the tree and new Easter outfits. I wanted that kind of life. It just seemed so much more carefree and it seemed to have no rules. I wanted in, and I shared this with one of my friends. To my surprise, she informed me I was already a Christian because Jesus died for my sins and because *all* Black people were Christians! For a moment I was a bit confused. I thought, "Wow, could this be so?" It wasn't what my uncle told me, or what my mother taught me, nor was it what I learned at Temple on Saturdays. I was taught that there was only one God and his name was not Jesus, nor was he a person, so he couldn't be seen, therefore he wasn't the guy in the picture or on the cross and he didn't have any "children" other than his first born son, Israel.

I loved going to Temple on Shabbat. We would get all dressed up and I would get my hair pressed and my mother would let me wear bangs. You just had to be there. It was wonderful. Services lasted all day Saturday, but it was okay. When we walked in the door of our temple I would take off my coat, my mother would tie a neatly folded scarf around my head and I would seek out my friends. I was always so happy to see them because they weren't like my other friends. I had something more in common with them than the kids I played with on my block. When the rabbi did the call to worship, everyone would hurry from where they were and stop whatever it was they were doing and file into the sanctuary, the men on one side, the women on the other. And all the children would sit together on a couple of pews. We were watched very closely by one of the sisters who still to this day can shoot me a look that will make me straighten up and fly right. There was no playing, talking or running around, and the only way you were going to the bathroom was if you were on the verge of drowning. In hindsight, it wasn't so bad.

I would look around at this group of people, my uncle and all the other men wearing their suits and ties with their kippot , the small cap that most Jewish men wear and white tallit, prayer shawls with shiny blue stripes and all the women wearing their Saturday dresses and head coverings and everyone listening attentively to the rabbi bringing the D'rasha (message), nodding their heads in agreement, and sometimes hollering out a Hallelujah, or an Amen to encourage the rabbi on and to let him know that what he was saying was important and actually touching someone. It was beautiful and I was proud to be a part of it. My favorite part was always the singing. The entire congregation sang together, the organist playing, and the tambourine ringing and the drummers pounding, and we would sing about how Canaan belonged to us. And as a child I had no idea what or where Canaan was, but I knew if it was this happy and they sang like this there, I would be more than happy to go. After services were over we ate a large meal together, and it always reminded me of Thanksgiving. There was a ton of food and everyone sat down together and over the meal everyone would catch up. They would share about what happened at work or a football game, about their children, about anything that had happened to them during the week. The children would eat fast and then we would finally get to play.

I loved to go home and share my experiences with my cousins. It didn't even matter if they wanted to hear it or not, I'd tell it anyway. Sometimes they'd get excited too and when we would have special events at temple, they would always come. I was very comfortable with who I was. I knew what I could and couldn't eat. I knew what days I went to pray. I knew those rules, the rules of *how* to be who I was, but most importantly, I knew exactly *who* I was, the little Ethiopian Israelite girl.

So I stood there, on April 11, 2008, staring in the mirror and eventually breaking down and crying. But I wasn't sad at all. I cried for so long because I was crying the tears of so many people. I was crying the tears of all of the people I saw in my face that morning. I was crying for my uncle who thought my identity–as a one of the Children of Israel, as an Israelite, as black Jew—was the most important thing in the world. I was crying for my grandmother, who allowed my mother and uncle to be who they were meant to be. I was crying for all of the ancestors who gave a piece of themselves to the people who would give pieces of themselves to me and who I in turn would pass on to my black Jewish daughter the very next day at her Baht Mitzvah. They were tears of joy, but even more, tears of gratitude.

CHAPTER 2

ETHIOPIA SHALL STRETCH HER HANDS UNTO GOD   כּוּשׁ תָּרִיץ יָדָיו לֵאלֹהִים

When I was five, it came time for me to go to school and by that time I thought I had a pretty good understanding of myself. It was 1983 and by that time I had seen Alex Haley's *Roots*, at least four or five times. I had been to Mississippi and I knew that's where my family came from and I knew that's where some of the people that were on the same ship as Kunta Kinte were sold off to. I also knew that Kunta Kinte was African and when he got here they made him a slave and then made him change his name to Toby. I had also heard many of my grandmother's stories about some of my ancestors who were slaves, so I felt like Toby's story might have been a lot like my own.

I had also seen Cecil B. DeMille's cinematic *masterpiece The Ten Commandments* many, many times. It was my favorite movie. There were beautiful actresses and opulent costumes, and there was Yul Brynner, who had the best legs I've ever seen on any man, and then there was the noble Moses. In the movie, Moses was played by a young Charleton Heston who was everything a child could want in a Biblical hero. However, after seeing Moses trade in Egypt for the Planet of the Apes and utter the words "from my cold dead hands" as an adult, he ceased to be my hero. But when I was a child, he was strong, handsome and a valiant deliverer of the Jewish people. It always made me especially proud, because growing up as an Israelite in a predominately non-Israelite household; *The Ten Commandments* was *my* story.

It was the story I learned about at Temple and the one my uncle taught me about, and it was also one that my grandmother would tell me over and over again. It was there on every single TV in our house in beautiful cinemascope, and sometimes even on Easter! The day may have been about Jesus, but for those four or five hours while everyone was glued to their televisions, it was all about Moses and the Children of Israel, which was me. Somehow, this movie gave validity to my religion.

I knew what was going to happen and why and how. I knew Moses' staff was gonna turn into a serpent and swallow up the serpent of Pharaoh. I knew that the Children of Israel were going to put blood on their doorposts. I knew that the sea was going to open up and that they were going to cross safely. I could tell all of the rest of the kids in my house everything that was going to happen scene by scene, but there was something else: I could also tell them what happened after Moses went into the mountain and was assumed to have died. Most importantly, I could tell them what made me the most proud: Egypt, the land which Moses led the Children of Israel out of was in Africa! Yes, Africa.

The same Africa that Kunta Kinte came from, and the same Africa that the slaves my Grandmother would talk about came from. So at the age of five I had to deduce that the Children of Israel (as I knew myself to be at that point) came from Africa! Right? They had to, because I knew where Egypt was on the map and I knew where black people came from and the two were one and the same. Furthermore, Egypt was right above Ethiopia, and I was my uncle's Ethiopian girl. This always made me so proud. Who I was, was so important that movies were made about it, movies about blacks and Israelites. I never paid attention to the fact that Levar Burton and Charleton Heston were both playing the roles of Africans, even though one was black and the other was white. This should have told me something, but I was five, and I would find out soon enough.

As the summer drew to a close, my mother explained that I would be going to a school that we would have to get on the bus to go to. The thought of going to a real school was exciting to me. I had been to a head start program, but that was only part of the day in a mobile classroom. It was full of the kids from my neighborhood and also one of my cousins. I went there to draw pictures and play, but the school that my mother was talking about was something altogether different. I got new school clothes and shoes and for the first time I got a backpack! She told me that it was kind of a long ride and there would be kids there that I didn't know, but I wouldn't alone; my friends from Temple would be there. I was downright giddy.

However, what she didn't tell me was that I'd be there all day and she wouldn't be there, and neither would Mama (my grandmother), and on top of that, there were a bunch of white people, something new for me. This was a shock. I can remember thinking how far away from home I must have been because of the long bus ride. My mind couldn't seem to process any of it. I was far from home, by myself, and the people that had been put in charge of taking care of me looked nothing like anyone who had ever taken care of me before. It was terrifying. This is when I experienced my first panic attack. My body tensed up, my chest got tight and it was hard to breathe. All of the fluids that leak from ones face when they're spazzing out had began dripping down my chin and on to my shirt. I was a tear soaked, snotty mess!

After a few hours in the office of the school secretary, a stern but sweet older lady who would eventually become very good friends with my grandmother, and after a whole bunch of Kleenex and cups of water, I was finally ready to go meet my new classmates.

As I walked through the cool, quiet gray hallways escorted by the secretary, the faint aroma of school paste in the air gave me a bit of comfort because it reminded me of the little mobile school house in my neighborhood where all the other black kids and my cousin were. As we walked down the hall, I can remember the only sound that could be heard was the shhh, shhh, shhh of my hair,coming from the colored beads braided into my hair clashing together as if it were my theme music. We stopped at a door and there was silence again, until the secretary opened the door. Then there was chaos and noise and kids running and playing and some sitting at tables and others over in the corner pretending to cook in a kitchen and even in my fear and apprehension it was familiar and so were a couple of the kids from my Temple, and it made me smile. Finally, I was relaxed enough to start the next phase of my life, kindergarten.

Despite my feeling of not belonging, I noticed there were Hebrew letters written on things and the male principal wore a kippah, the little cap that men at my Temple wore. I knew what that was. It was what my uncle and every other black man at my Temple wore because they were Israelites. I also noticed the little boys in my class were wearing them too. I didn't say anything at that moment, too involved with coloring, cutting and gluing, but soon it was time to put things away and clean up for snack time. I knew what that was because we had had it at my old school. It wasn't long before everyone had done their part and was hungry and thirsty.

We sat as patiently as kindergartners could, anticipating our snack. That day we had animal crackers and Hi-c red punch from the can. As the teachers went around making sure everyone got theirs, they also told us not to eat or drink yet. I sat there and waited, and once everyone had their snack, the teacher lifted her cup and motioned for us all to do the same and what she would say next almost knocked me off of my seat, She began to pray: B'ruch atah a'donai eloheinu melech ha'olam boray pri hagafen, amen. That was *my* prayer! It was the prayer we said at Temple and at home before the adults drank wine and we drank juice! She didn't stop there. She then went on to make Ha'motzi, the blessing over the cookies, another prayer that I did at Temple and at home.

I was really confused at this point. How did she and the other students know those prayers? They weren't all black and they didn't go to my Temple, and if my cousins who all lived in the same house with me and were black couldn't learn them, how and why could these people? And why were the boys wearing kippot? I had to know. There were black kids, white kids, a couple of biracial kids, and even a real Ethiopian kid, and all of them wore kippot. As we sat there eating and drinking, I finally raised my hand. The teacher turned to me and smiled."Yes, Tamar?" I took a deep breath and looked at the kids in my class once again and then said, "Why are the boys wearing a kippah, and why did you say that prayer?"

There, I said it! It was out there. She smiled and said, "Because we are Jewish." What? Jewish? What was that? I was an Israelite, one of the Children of Israel. The only thing I knew about Jews when I was five was that there was a part of Chicago that was called Jew Town where people would go to buy stuff for cheap. She went on to explain that we were all Jews because we believed the same things, no matter what we called ourselves. Just because I called myself something different didn't mean that I wasn't a Jew. So, from that day forward I was known as a Jew. I guess it was ok. And at the end of the day, I went home and I told my uncle that we were Jews.

Like so many Israelites at that time, he did not like that name at all. He asked me, who told you that you were a Jew? I went on to explain to him that my teacher had told me that we were all Jews and that my school was a Jewish school and that there were kids of all different ethnicities and colors and we were all Jews. He looked at me and said, "You are who you are." Then he asked the question, "If we are all the same, then why do you have to start calling yourself a Jew, instead of them calling themselves Israelites?" It was a fair question. He had a way of making everything he said sound perfectly logical.

My uncle and other Israelites had come into this way of life at a much different time from the one we were living in then. There were very strong Black Nationalist undertones in their religious thought. They called themselves Israelites or Children of Israel and in the 1960's and 70's, a new black identity was emerging and it was one that said: I am going to be self-determining and I do not want to be associated with anything that is white. Blacks weren't going to call themselves Jews because white people did; they would be Israelites or Hebrew Israelites.

My uncle made it a point to ask me every day when I came home from school about what I had learned that day, and the more he asked, the more I wanted to learn. I was excited to come home and discuss the new Bible story I'd learned or a new word I'd learned to write. It was as though he and I were learning together, and he taught me other things as well. He stayed on top of my education. The teachers at school would tell me one thing, I'd come home, and he would listen and often rebut it. He gave me teachings on their teachings, providing me with balance. He never allowed me to lose myself in the world of the Jews. I would come home and share with him lessons that I had learned from the Torah that day and he would pull out book after book to show me the African presence in the same lesson or our relevance. He could make anything about *me* and he did. As much as he often disagreed with the lessons my teachers tried to teach me at school, he still felt like my being there was important. I learned years later that it was so important to him that he helped my mother pay my tuition, even though he was on a fixed income. He wanted to me to learn whatever it was that Jews knew, especially their language. He was convinced that Hebrew had been stolen from us and that in rediscovering our language, I would recover other parts of myself that lay hidden.

So I went to school and learned how to be a good Jew. There were many families at my Temple, but there were so many more at white synagogues (another new word for me). There were Jewish people everywhere, far more than I had ever imagined. They were in my classroom, they were my teachers, and they were war heroes and philanthropists that gave money to the poor, even to poor black people. They were rich and they came from places like Russia, Poland, and Hungary, but what stuck out the most was they were white, every single last one of them. By the time I got to first grade, the only black Jews I knew were the ones at my Temple and in my family.

I would sit in class and listen to the kids talk about their grandparents, their Bubbe and Zette, in Yiddish. They had stories that had been passed down in their families that traced their Jewish lineage. They were Reform, Conservative , and Reconstructionist . I wasn't sure what I was. There were those who talked about their ancestors arriving at Ellis Island and then there were those who told heartbreaking stories of family who did and didn't survive the Holocaust. They spoke of family traditions and going away to visit family in other states for Passover or Yom Kippur. But not me or any of the other black kids in my class. We didn't have stories like that.

Our stories were about being black, not Jewish. We didn't have an Ellis Island because we came from places like Mississippi, Alabama, and the Carolinas. We were the descendants of slaves whose names most of us didn't know. Our ancestors were bought over in chains in the hulls of ships, riddled with disease and death; they never stared out at Lady Liberty from the deck of a steamship and dreamed of the better life she might offer them. We were poor. We all had parents who struggled to pay our tuition. There were no trips to visit family for holy days. Who could afford it, and who would we visit? We had few Jewish family members and only a brief history as Jews. They could trace their ancestors back centuries and in their family trees had been rabbis and sofers, (scribes) and even a gaon, a sage, but most of us could only trace our Jewish roots back to our parents. Most of our grandparents weren't Israelites, and who knew what our ancestors had been?

It made me sad and embarrassed and a bit jealous. They all seemed liked better Jews than I was. They knew all the rules and the words to the songs and stories that I didn't know. They did things the Jewish way, like not eating meat and milk together as I did. Some of the girls didn't wear pants like I did. They were mostly European Jews, so they even had their own language in addition to the Hebrew that we were all learning together. It almost made me doubt that I was a Jew at all. I didn't envy their money or whiteness, or even their culture, but I did envy the fact that they had a history.

Sure, I had been taught that the Children of Israel came out of Egypt, which was in Africa, and I knew that's where black people came from, but somewhere between Timbuktu and Englewood my history got lost. It seemed to me that at the same time mine seemed to be falling into obscurity, theirs was coming into prominence. In the midst of it all, I still knew who I was, thanks to my uncle. For my entire grade school career my uncle and I discussed and debated, and the more I learned at school, the more he taught me, even though sometimes I didn't like his lessons.

By the third grade I had begun to assimilate. All I wanted to do was be a Jew, like all the other Jews. I was tired of people asking me how I was a Jew and the awkward conversations that followed. I had learned to give the politically correct answers and not the more controversial, philosophical and more truthful ones that I had learned from my uncle. I was exhausted and I just wanted to be left alone. I hated having to justify my blackness to black people and my Jewishness to the Jewish folk. I was tired of fighting for myself and defending my identity all the time. I was grateful to the Jews at school for not questioning my Judaism and making me explain myself. I was happy they let me be a Jew, just like everyone else. They knew me, so they never had to ask. I was exactly what they told me I was: a Jew.

As I settled into my new school, I began to see the difference between my neighborhood and the one that my school was in, and I also began to notice that the problems my neighborhood didn't exist in those of the other children at school. They came from several affluent areas of the city and the suburbs. They worried about stuff like who would come to their piano and violin recitals, and as much as I would've loved to take music lessons, my mother couldn't afford it. They worried about if their dog would be hurt at the groomer; I couldn't have a dog because there was no room in my house. Yet, I wasn't resentful. They were my friends and I lived vicariously through them. Some of the kids

17

were really nice. I enjoyed hearing about things that I'd never experienced and seeing pictures from their vacations and going to sleepovers in places that I could only dream of one day living in. I had gotten to the point where I had become so agreeable that I allowed my teacher to literally take my name and give it to another student.

There was a girl who came to my school from another country when I was in the third grade and her Hebrew name was Tamar. However, Tamar was my name all the time. It was what my mother named me. It was both my Hebrew and English name, and suddenly this girl's name was Tamar too. The teachers thought would the fair solution would be to take my name and add the Hebrew letter HAY to the end, making my name Tamarah and making her Tamar. It was a big deal to me. Tamar was *my* name, and when they took it from me, it hurt. I never complained about it and since my mother couldn't read Hebrew, she didn't notice that for an entire year I spelled my name differently. I had truly started to become someone else, someone who just went along to get along. I felt better once the school year was over and Tamar left the school and I got to be myself again.

It was all a wonderful lie until one day a girl a bit older than me made a comment that would change my life forever. It wasn't exactly what she said; it was the way she said it. The comment seethed with contempt, and at that moment we were no longer all Jews; for the first time at that school, in the only color blind place I had known, I became aware that some Jews who were white taught their children the exact same things about black people that many other white people did.

I had thought that they were different, but at that moment I learned that they weren't, and neither was I. What my family said at home when I would profess how much my "friends" loved me was true: fat meat really was greasy. They were who I was told they were.

Perhaps the parents of some of the children at my school had said things around the dinner table that led their children to believe the stereotypes about black people that other whites did. This is when I learned that we could never really be friends because they pitied me because I was poor and black and I really *wanted* to be a Jew, or they were nice to me because black people were angry and barbaric and I might beat them up.

I tried that role out for a while and I became the tiniest bully the world had ever seen. I began to terrorize even the biggest of boys and they would always cower in fear. It wasn't because I scared them; it was because they had already been taught to fear me. I just learned to exploit it. This was a turning point in my life. I was no longer one of them when I was at school. I had changed. In that change I began re-evaluating myself and I noticed that in the process of my trying to be one of *them* at school, I had begun rejecting other parts of *me*.

In my neighborhood, there was plenty of crime and violence and I had tried to turn a blind eye to it because my school, the place where I spent the majority of my time, was far away across town. I could come home from school and go into my house and stay there until it was time to escape my neighborhood again the next day, but suddenly, I felt I didn't have that option anymore. The truth was, I was one of "them." I was one of the people who I hid from, who I never invited for a sleep-over because I didn't want to see our similarities. I had to learn that it was okay to be in, but not of. I started to listen to my far more militant Uncle Larry preach endlessly about the politics of our people and how we needed to change and how we could change if we just cared more. I was familiar with politics and I had heard his passionate and never ending rants on political matters, and now I began to pay attention. This was the uncle who took me out to campaign for Harold Washington in the cold when I was five years old. He taught me the meaning of civic responsibility. I was discovering yet another side of myself. I was still an Israelite, but I wasn't a Jew, or at least not the kind of Jew I knew at school. I was no longer a part of their club. I wasn't their best friend anymore. I was there to learn about Judaism, but not allowed to be a Jew in the same way they were.

Ironically, my school was right across the street from the home of Harold Washington, Chicago s first black mayor, and I knew him. He was Harold. He was a man of the people. Had it not been for Harold, the idea of a Barack Obama becoming President would never have been. He ignited a fire in the Black people of Chicago, and for the first time we flexed our political muscle and elected a black man as mayor in 1983. This nearly tore the city apart. The racism that many parts of Chicago had become famous for began to surface once again. There was a body formed by members of the Chicago city council which con-sisted of ethnic whites and also sowed dissension. This body was called, Vrodolyak s 29 , because it was led by Alderman Ed. Vrodolyak. This group created all sorts of mayhem, especially legislative gridlock. When

I watch the news now, I tell ya , it s like déjà vu all over again! Chicago became infamous for its city council wars and would be dubbed Beirut on the lake . Even in the face of this opposition, he persevered. He had an amazing team behind him that included blacks, hispanics and Jews. He was willing to work with anyone who was willing to work with him. He was the pride of black Chicago. It was the beginning of a new era in Chicago, and the city stood behind Mayor Washington and supported his programs. They rewarded him by re-electing him for a second term on April 8, 1987. I was in the fourth grade then. He died that year some say he was poisoned–the day before Thanksgiving.

I was at school when it happened and I had seen him that morning on his way to City Hall as I had so many mornings. He seemed fine, and then he was gone. As the news spread around the school, the reaction of the some of the other kids bothered me. There were many liberal families there, but apparently it wasn't as many as I had believed. Some of the children were nearly in tears as we watched the news in the teachers' lounge, but some laughed and rejoiced that he was dead. I was inconsolable. Harold was gone, and with him the new-found pride and the hopes and dreams of black Chicago. Just as there had never been a joy in the black community like the night that Harold was elected, there has since been no sorrow like the day he died.

I went back to school after the holiday break and I did not forget the ones who laughed. I was unfriendly to them and I began experimenting with my boundaries: things I could say, things I could do. The less I tried to fit in and be nice and please everyone all the time, the more I became who I really was. I was able to disagree with people I didn't agree with. I was no longer keeping my head down and walking softly. I was learning to assert myself and I liked it.

The summer before fifth grade, my grandmother died. I didn't know how much she meant until she was gone. My grandmother had raised me and been my companion for nearly my entire life. My mother was single and she had two daughters, a job, and school to attend. She came home after I was asleep and she left for work just when I came home from school, so we missed each other a lot. It was my grandmother who was there for me in a way my mother couldn't be. She got me up every morning and warm-combed my incredibly coarse hair. She bathed, dressed and fed me, took me to school and picked me up every day, and she was never late.

The bus time was our time to talk. She would talk and talk and tell me all kinds of stuff. My grandmother was my bridge between the old world and the new. In addition to teaching me how to dispose of hair from the straightening comb, and making sure I always had on clean underwear, in case I had an accident, of course. Her stories were her true legacy. In a time when we were being introduced to the vcr and music videos, my grandmother was telling me true stories about how she had a great grandmother in North Carolina that was sold off the day before Lincoln Emancipated the slaves. Her new owners hadn't had time to take her far. She was able to be reunited with her family. She also told me about things that weren't so happy, like how she was rejected by her uncle who was a minister. Her mother had left her and she went to stay with a great aunt who had children of her own. Her aunt loved her as if she were here own and all of the children called each other "sister". However, when the depression came and times got too hard she didn't have enough money to care for my Grandmother anymore. She turned to her brother who was well off and supposedly a man of God, but he shunned her. In front of my Grandmother, when she was only a child, he said he couldn't take a Bastard into his house! After that she would go from home to home, pillar to post, never having a stable place to lay her head, until she was 15, when she married my Grandfather. I believe she shared the things that she felt had most shaped her life and she felt that even at the present, they still had value. It was often adult talk; I think she knew I wouldn't have her for long, so she tried to give me all she could while she could. I was her shadow. And when she died, I wasn't used to doing anything alone because I never had. But now it was time for me to learn.

I was ten when school started back in the fall. I took the bus across town all by myself for the first time. I was never afraid because I knew mama was with me. Even as she is now. Independence suited me; if I could go to school by myself, I could do everything by myself. It was a big deal to be the only kid at school who was allowed to take the bus alone. I felt grown up. Soon after, I got my first babysitting job and you couldn't tell me nothing! Others were starting to see that I was growing up too, and I was proud of myself.

I was light years ahead of the other fifth graders, and it's typical even now for black children to have to grow up and assume some sort of responsibility sooner than other children. But as my life was changing, so were the lives of everyone in my family. My grandmother's death had taken an immense toll on our family and we began to fall apart. There were fights and arguments and disputes over bills. There was alcoholism and drug addiction, everyone looking for a way to cope with the pain of losing Mama. She had held us all together, and now that she was gone, we were coming unglued. When I was twelve, my mother moved out of her mother's house and away from her sisters and brothers for the first time in her life. I would never be the same again; nothing would ever be the same again.

In the midst of my personal upheaval, the black community was going through its own growing pains. In 1989, Spike Lee released *Do the Right Thing* and Public Enemy was telling us to fight the power, while N.W.A. made me want to be a Nigga with an Attitude. But I was stuck in Jewish day school. By this time I was in full rebellion. The breakup of the family had hit me hard, and I found no comfort in things that previously had steadied me. I hardly ever went to Temple and I didn't live in the same house with my uncle anymore, and I was more into being black than being a Jew. My teachers talked about things that were no longer true to me. I had learned from KRS -1 that Kush was Ethiopia. Why had they never taught me that in school? And why would they not acknowledge the fact that Egypt was in Africa, or that the Children of Israel were black, or that the Middle East was something invented in the 20th Century? I watched the news and listened to my uncle Larry, the radical and read books. I was acutely aware of what was going on in the world and I saw that much of it related to me. It began to drive me crazy that the rest of the kids didn't seem to care about what they were being taught; they cared about grades instead. I was insulted by what I was being taught, and even more by what they would not teach like how awful the Rodney King beating was or why America really invaded Iraq just to name a few things that absolutely galled me. I was angry. My grades begin to drop and so did my respect for my classmates and teachers. I couldn't do it anymore. I left Jewish day school in the middle of the seventh grade. It would be years before I would return.

CHAPTER 3

BARUCH HABAH WELCOME   בָּרוּךְ הַבָּא

The joy that I found in just the thought of sitting in a classroom full of black kids cannot be expressed in words. I was so excited that I had laid my clothes out, sharpened my pencils, put paper in my binder and bought an apple for my teacher a week before winter break was over. Finally, I was going to be in a place where *who* I was mattered. I would be in a place where I could be cool because I always had the newest Air Jordans and the latest Starter coat. My jeans were all designer and it seemed as if I could go months without wearing the same thing twice. It wasn't because my mother spoiled me, but because I lived in a house with an older sister and cousins who were constantly coming and going and everybody could fit everybody else's stuff. This was going to make me the wo-"MAN" at school because where we lived now, no one could afford to dress like that. At my Jewish school they had no sense of style. I could wear new Jordans every day and no one would even notice. They wore Vans, maybe, or Kmart brands and maybe even sometimes hand me downs. I'd finally be somewhere that respected how truly fly I really was, and it wouldn't hurt that I'd have black teachers, who got it. I couldn't wait to be in a place where I didn't have to watch what I said or my the use of my "provocative language" wouldn't get me in trouble. I could finally just be me.

The night before school started right after the first of the new year, which was 1990. I asked my mother if she would curl my hair. I probably didn't ask her as nicely as I should have; there was nothing nice about me at that time.

After my Grandmother died we had to move from the only home that any of us had ever known. Once Mama was gone, my mother, aunts and uncles showed themselves to be her children. When she was alive they were on their best behavior and I don't even think they realized it, but when my grandmother died, everything her watchful eye kept bottled up inside of them overflowed. There were constant fights, not like arguments, but real exchanges of blows. It became so bad that had they all stayed together in that house, someone would've been killed. After the fights were over and everybody was calm again and I was done crying, I thought I was okay. I thought all us kids were okay, but we weren't and we would never be. I believe it was because my mother was a Psychology major in college, that she knew we weren't okay and that we were somehow being damaged even if it wasn't apparent how at the time. Since she couldn't afford counseling for the entire family, she took my sister and me and moved closer to my school, but not close enough.

We moved to a building that was half of step above the projects and that only because there were fewer units. It was made of cement and cinderblock and the floors were concrete. The rooms were small, and for the first time in my life, we had roaches. My grandmother had hated them and so did we all. Even though her house had been filled to the rafters with people, we had never had roaches. If we ever did see one in our house it was discussed whose guest it was that carried it in. After that my grandmother would find a polite way to stand them on the front porch and shake them and their belongings out prior to coming into our house. My mother and aunts never learned that kind of tact.

Besides that, the new place wasn't that bad. For the first time, my sister and I had a bedroom all to ourselves. I suppose that was the only thing that made the roaches bearable. At first I was a little homesick. I missed the constant noise in my grandmother's overcrowded house. Even now I marvel at how my grandmother managed to find room for cousins, friends, and sometimes even strangers who had nowhere to go. I can't remember anybody sleeping in the bathtub, but just because I can't remember it doesn't mean it didn't happen. There was always noise and the smell of somebody cooking and the door opening and closing and footsteps on the porch, but here there was nothing. We lived on the eighth floor, so there was no porch. The floors weren't wood, so there were no creaking floorboards and most of the time there was nobody there but me, so there was no sound of voices. I missed my grandmothers house and my family. But we had to move, because my mother said so.

My Grandmother used to get me dressed and take me to school and do everything I needed while my mother was at work, but now I was stuck with her. It was weird; I knew she was my mother and that she loved me, but she cooked foods I didn't like and asked questions I thought she should've known the answers to. She didn't because she didn't really know me, or at least not like my grandmother did. I made her pay for being a single mom, and the better a mom she tried to be, the harder I went on her. My grades dropped, my attitude changed, and I was purposefully mean to her. I thought it was okay, but as my Grandmother used to say, "Just keep livin".

My mother stood there curling my hair in silence. She was angry and hurt that I was going to the neighborhood school that all of the kids in the building, my new "friends", went to. She asked me only one question when she was finished with my hair: "Are you happy?" I didn't respond. I didn't know if she meant was I happy with my hair or if I was happy that I finally got my way in going to the new school. My hair was fine, but I honestly didn't know how to respond to the other question. I didn't know; school hadn't started yet. Would I be as smart as the other kids, would I be as cool, would they like me? My mother's question made me nervous and self-conscious and I had just found a new reason to be mad at her.

I think I was up and dressed by 5 a.m. but I didn't dare arrive at school on time because I didn't want to look desperate. When I finally got to school-late-my heart pounded as I walked through the door, but you couldn't tell from my look. I was wearing the latest everything, my hair was perfect, and I had an Eddie Bauer backpack. I was certain to be the envy of every boy and girl in my class and the knowledge of that drowned out the flapping of the butterflies' wings in my stomach. I walked into the classroom and I nearly stopped in my tracks. It looked like an invading army encamped in there. It amazed me to see so many kids packed into one classroom; at my old school this would've been an assembly! It didn't deter me though. I was ready. There were a few kids from my apartment building in my class and some others from around my new neighborhood, which afforded an extra degree of comfort.

I sat down and was ready to learn. I couldn't wait to hear the truth. I couldn't wait to hear my teacher, who was white, share with me all of the things that the teachers at my Jewish day school never would. She bought me an American History book, an English book and a Math book. All of them were old, but the history book looked the oldest. The constant re-taping made it look ready for the trash but I wasn't going to complain. This was my new school and I was ready to learn, and learn I did.

The first week of school was eventful. There were a lot of firsts. There was my first gym class. There was the first time I witnessed a fist fight at school and there was the first time I ate in a lunch room that wasn't kosher. I was used to bringing my own lunch from home, but I figured I didn't have to do that anymore because this was a new school and things were different. I can remember getting in the lunch line one day during that first week and having the guy behind the lunch counter scoop up a ladle of beans and dump them on my tray. As I moved down the line I overheard someone say the words pork and beans. I was hungry, but the words pork and beans killed my appetite. This was the first time I was ever offered anything that I couldn't eat when I was actually hungry, and no one was around to enforce the rules. My decision to not eat this thing that I knew to be unclean was the first Jewish thing I did after leaving my previous school. I wanted to be cool so I told the other kids in my class I couldn't eat it because school lunches were gross and they weren't fit for human consumption, not even the nachos. My convincing them that I was too cool for school lunch led to a year of me swapping my lunch for the adoration of any kid who I saw fit to award it to that day.

I learned another very important lesson at lunch: I was too skinny for a black girl! One day while sitting at lunch with a group of friends, a boy stood up and proclaimed in front of the entire lunchroom that if I had another girl's body and she had my face, we would both be beautiful! This bothered me on a level that I had never quite experienced before. For the first time, I was self conscious about the way I looked. I had come from a place where black was black; no one saw shades, and no one ever paid attention to the fact that I was small, because all of the girls in my old school were small! I was the average size of a thirteen year old, but not a thirteen year old black girl. After that, the girl who he compared me to was no longer my friend and I wore jogging pants under everything for the next four years to appear "thicker".

There were different cliques of girls here, very much unlike my old school. There simply hadn't been enough girls there for social divisions there, but there were plenty here. I didn't fit in with any of them, even though I tried. There were the light skinned girls, the smart but less attractive girls, who all seemed to be dark skinned, and there were the gang banging girls who everyone was afraid of. I didn't know how to fit in, in any of these groups. In a place where I had figured we were all the same, I was still different. I wouldn't eat the same food as the other kids. I had proven myself to be smart by dominating class discussions on things I thought everyone knew but didn't. I was pretty, but I wasn't light skinned, yet I was too light to be accepted by the dark-skinned girls.

My mother had a different mentality from many of the parents of the other kids there. I didn't think it was cool to curse at the teacher, and when other kids would do it, I would be embarrassed. I didn't want my teachers to think I was like that. I had more nice things than the other kids did, and I thought that would make them love me, but it only bred jealousy and jealousy bred something else: hatred. By March I was persona non grata. I had friends, but they were mostly boys and that made matters no better for me. Boys were never jealous of my clothes or my shoes or my face because they were guys, and I would soon find out that most of them were into something totally different.

I got good grades at my new school for a while and then I stopped caring once again. The realization that they taught even less about black people in a black school than they did in a white one shook me to my core. That may have been bad, but what was worse was the fact that they taught less of everything in this new school. The kids were blissfully ignorant. They had no idea what was going on in the books and they didn't care. At one point I thirsted for acceptance so badly that I would let them cheat off of my papers and I knew that was wrong. I knew all of it was wrong. The cheating, the trying to fit in, the attitude, all of it was wrong and I knew it was wrong because I was a Jew and I had not been raised that way. I knew what trying to fit in had gotten me before and that I should honor my mother and not abuse her, I knew my commandments. I should have remembered the lesson that I was taught in a history class at my old school. The Jews in Europe who dared to assimilate were persecuted by those who they sought to emulate and ostracized by those in the community they tried their best to distance themselves from. That was me. I was that Jew. I did things to fit in only afterwards to be wracked with guilt and the shame they came with it. I knew that I wasn't like everybody else even though I wanted to be so badly. I found myself alone again.

I was in a new school and I was living in a new place and I had to learn new lessons that didn't much seem like they were worth learning, but if I were going to survive in my new world, I had to. I didn't know if I'd be like some of the women in my building, trapped here with my children and no husband to help. I didn't know. It really got scary when one of my friends who had just turned fourteen had a baby. What do fourteen-year-olds buy other fourteen years olds for baby shower gifts? Whatever their ten buck a week allowances will get them. I could remember what she was like when she was a kid, just like me, but now she was somebody's mother and I couldn't relate.

My mother made it clear that we would not be there forever. It was temporary until we could find somewhere nicer. My mother worked and went to school every day and while she was at school and work I began to go and hide out at my Uncle David's house, waiting for the time to come for us to move. My Uncle David and his family had moved down the street from us, but it was in a better part of the neighborhood and only a couple of blocks away from my old school. I loved being there. I could just relax. The building was full of college students and professionals and very few kids. It sat in a park-like setting, so I would go outside and take walks and read my books under the trees, not worried about anything at all. My building, which was only eight blocks away, was in a whole different galaxy. I was happy at David's, but still quite lonely.

I lived in a new place and so did my uncle. I went to a new school. I never had friends in the neighborhood until now, and I had even cut my hair off. What a difference a year makes. I know I must have been a stranger to all of those that knew me because I had become a stranger to myself. I was lying to my mother and my uncle. I was doing things that I knew I shouldn't have been doing, but I needed friends, and if that meant being with people doing things my mother and uncle wouldn't approve of, at least I wasn't doing them alone.

I began waking up on Saturday mornings feeling sad because I knew I shouldn't be sleeping until noon or going shopping or hanging out with my friends. I should've been at Temple. Little things reminded me every day that I was still a Jew, and I missed the freedom to be one.

Shortly after I turned fourteen, I decided that I wanted to go and visit with my old friends from Temple and from school. We still talked on the phone sometimes, but we lived in different parts of the city so we never saw each other anymore. I was old enough to take the bus now as long as I told my mother first. One Saturday morning, I got a feeling that I hadn't felt in a long time. I was happy I was going to service. I wasn't going to wear gym shoes and jeans today. I was going to wear a skirt and some tights and a pair of my mother's dress shoes. Sure, I was going to comb my hair, but no one was going to see it because it would be hidden under my neatly-tied scarf. This all felt so familiar and so good.

I had to walk four blocks and take three busses to get there, but I didn't mind because I was going to Temple. The closer I got the more my heart raced. I felt like I was coming home after a long trip. I got off the bus and as I walked up the block I could see a giant Star of David glinting in the sun over the trees. It was impossible to miss. I was so hurried to get to my Temple that I paid no mind to the people and the dangers that may have lurked in the streets that surrounded it. Finally, I arrived at the gates adorned by two golden lions of Judah. I swung them open and walked up the three short stairs to the door, and as I opened it, I held my breath.

What if I don't remember the prayers? What if everybody knows how much I have changed? What if God makes me burst into flames when I walk in the door? These were the thoughts racing through my head, but in moments I was already in the vestibule and the door had closed behind me. I stood there and looked around. This place was old, very old. It was a little dark and kind of damp and chilly, but it had a feeling to it. I could feel that people had prayed there for many years; perhaps it was the residue of all of the prayers that had gone up and out in that place over the years that cast what seemed to be a fog that played in the light of the stained glass window atop the door, or it could've been the familiar smoke of the burning frankincense. Whatever it was, for the first time in a long time I felt as if I belonged.

As I stood there, a man poked his head out of the closed doors at the top of the stairs and greeted me: "Shabbat Shalom." I returned the greeting and quietly walked up the stairs. I didn't know the gentleman, but he was very nice. As I stepped into the sanctuary, he gave me a Pentateuch and a Siddur, which were the "penta", five books of Moses and a prayer book. I took them and went to sit down. There were people there, but not many that I recognized. They said Amen in all of the right places and they seemed to understand everything that the rabbi was saying. I realized that just as I didn't recognize them, they didn't recognize me. I quietly slid into a pew where no one else was sitting and waited for the page on which everyone was reading was announced.

As I peered at the words on the page, it all started to come back to me and I began to join the harmony with the rest of the congregation. "Yours, Hashem, is the greatness, the strength, the splendor, the triumph and the glory, even everything in Heaven and Earth," I sang out, but the words didn't come from the same place that all of my other words came from. Those words meant nothing, and these did.

Everyday words came from a place that is not hard to get to and that's visited far too often, but these words came from a place inside of me that I wasn't even aware existed anymore. The turmoil of the past four years, the death of my Grandmother, the move, the new school had taken me far away from this place. A place I truly needed to be and now I was back and my heart was singing, "a song, a psalm for the Shabbat day," and it was so good to thank Hashem! My words came from the place that God put inside of me that allows me to connect with him and he to connect with me, and we hadn't connected this way in a very long time. I felt a lot of things at that moment, but mostly it was sadness. I had missed this part of my life and hadn't even known it. For years I had deprived myself of going to this *place,* and it made me sad. Here in this moment I felt God all around me as if he were reminding me of how things used to be, when I was a kid, when I was safe and protected and I had rules and boundaries. I thought I had come to see my friends, but they weren't the real reason. My soul knew what I needed even though my mind didn't.

I started going to service nearly every Shabbat now, most of the time I was by myself. My mother worked and so did my sister, and my uncle's medical condition kept him bedridden. But I wasn't alone long. Eventually, I became like everyone's daughter or sister. I got a new Imi and Abi or Mom and Dad. They were a couple who took me in and claimed me as their own, and to this day they are still my Imi and Abi. They were wonderful and Imi and I had a very spiritual connection. They were a couple that had come from another Israelite community in New York. They broadened my view of our culture. They were Israelites but somehow they were different. They knew all of the same prayers we did but they had different melodies and rhythms. Imi, too abided by the dress code of no pants and mandatory head coverings for women but hers were different. She would wear long beautifully colored garments made of African fabrics or Indian garments like sari's and salwaa chemise, those were my favorites. She had long locs that she would twist up and wrap in a cloth that always matched her outfits or wear them cascading down her back with scarf neatly and modestly, hiding them. I wanted to dress like her, be like her, because it just looked like she owned and understood her culture and after the confusion I had experienced, I needed to see that.

There were also those at my Temple who challenged my intellect. They had heard that I had attended Hebrew school, and they expected things of me. They would speak Hebrew to me and have philosophical discussions with me reminiscent of the conversations my uncle and I would have when I was a little girl. They gave me books to read and they never assumed I didn't know something. They always spoke to me in a way that I understood. Every Shabbat they would heap information on me. It didn't matter how outrageous my hair, my clothes or even my actions were, they still saw something in me that was valuable, and it gave me strength.

While I was away, my Temple had merged with others, taking the name Beth Shalom B'nai Zaken Ethiopian Hebrew Congregation. It was quite a mouthful. Each congregation brought something new to the table. Beth Shalom was old and that was where our rabbi began. B'nai Zaken were a newer group that grew out of the Black Power movement of the 60's, and the Ethiopian Hebrews was where the old met the new in Rabbi Abihu Reuben, who had been ordained a Rabbi in 1947, by Chief Rabbi Wentworth M. Matthew who was once the Chief Rabbi of the every black Jewish community in the western hemisphere, and Rabbi Capers C. Funnye our current Rabbi who was ordained in 1982, didn't become the head Rabbi until 1991 when Rabbi Reuben passed away at age 89. Rabbi Reuben was a very old man when I met him as a child, but even in his old age his stature and bellowing voice still commanded respect. He was the oldest black person that I'd ever known to read Hebrew. I had been under the impression that all older people were like the elders in my family: Christians with very little higher education, if any. Rabbi Reuben was different. As old as he was, he had a teacher even older, and that meant black Jews had been around longer than I had previously thought. He embodied the Ethiopian Hebrew, which my rabbi said didn't mean we were from Ethiopia, but that our minds and spirits had to be like hers: never conquered and always strong. That's who Ethiopia was and is.

It came to my attention at this time that our congregation had now been joined with other Israelite communities in other parts of the country, mainly in New York, and this also helped open my eyes to something greater. There were more of us than I knew. Other Jews had songs and traditions and their own culture, but so did we. Theirs was unique to their community, and so was ours. We were all a testimony to the diversity of Judaism.

I was still a teenager and now I was more conflicted than ever. I had a firm grasp of right and wrong and an active conscience. I got myself up on Shabbat morning, got dressed and went to service without any direction from my mother. I took responsibility for all my actions, even the bad ones. I struggled with the same things that other teens did: sex, drugs, rap music and peer pressure. I even almost got a tattoo once, but at the last minute I feigned hemophilia or something and got the heck outta there . Sometimes I would succumb to the *yetzer ha'rah*, the evil inclination. Even though I knew what it was to live a moral life, sometimes I had to learn the hard way. Like the time I was in the car with a guy who was way too old for me when he nearly got car jacked or robbed or potentially worse. Ironically, the only thing that saved our lives was the fact he had ran through a stop sign before we got to the light where we were sitting. This brought out the police. The sirens and lights scared the shooters off. I have never been so happy under such horrible circumstances. This point in my life was a great deal like what my uncle went through when he became an Israelite. The same family that I had thought made peace with the religious differences that existed within our family, really hadn't. People didn't treat me the same, and on more than one occasion I was accused of being in a cult. All week I could do and say and be whatever I wanted, but on Shabbat,

I wasn't Tammy: I was Tamar, and I looked forward to it. There was no arguing with my mother, no worry about whether I was pretty enough, or if a boy really liked me, or about a girl who wanted to fight me. Those things didn't exist in Temple and there I could be who I wanted to be all the time: an Israelite.

My mother asked me if I was trying to make all of my mistakes at once so I could get them all out of the way. It was the summer before my senior year and I was pregnant with my first child. I was supposed to be a good Jewish girl and I was supposed to know better because I had gone to private school. Many people had made sacrifices so I would have a better life. When I got pregnant, I disappointed a lot of people. At first I told my mother, but I hid it from my family for as long as I could. It was unacceptable and when they finally found out, they let me know it. One day my aunt told me that it was a good thing that my grandmother was already dead because the news would have killed her. My uncle David cried and my family mourned for me as if I had died. They all blamed my mother for the situation that I had created for myself, but it wasn't her fault. I was a smart girl or so I thought. I knew the consequences of unprotected sex and I was lucky that all I got was a baby. I knew right from wrong and while it would've been a whole lot easier to let her take the blame for what I had done, it wouldn't have been right. I thought perhaps the person who they loved and thought I was *had* died, and the new Tammy was on her own. I began to shut everyone else out while shutting myself in. I was ashamed. I didn't want anyone to see me. I was sad all of the time and the sight of my protruding stomach in the mirror made me sick. I even stopped going to Temple because I couldn't live with the embarrassment; there were those who had hopes and dreams and expectations of me, and I didn't have the heart to let them down. I felt alone, that I was nothing, and after this I could never be anything. Then one day it dawned on me that I was going to have a baby and that meant I was going to be a mother, and in my solitude I had nothing to do but think about what that meant. It came to me that I had been mothered more than most people I knew. I had a mother and a grandmother and aunts and more mothers and aunts at my Temple and if I could take a little bit of inspiration from each of them, I could do this. I could redeem myself by being a good mother I knew that babies needed to be taken care of. I'd have to buy milk and diapers and there would be doctors'

appointments and sleepless nights. I knew that she or he needed attention and lots of love, but what I knew the baby would need more than
anything was a strong relationship with God. I knew that if it were a
boy, he'd have to be circumcised on the eighth day and that if it were
a girl she'd have to have a naming ceremony. Despite the mess I had
made of my life, if I never let my children go, they would turn out fine.
I was eighteen then and I didn't think ahead to the day my own kid
would become a teenager.

Yom Kippur fell on October 16 of 1995, and it was also the day
the Nation of Islam-led Million Man March assembled on the National
Mall in Washington, D.C. I was in awe of such an assembly of black men
on my television. The entire neighborhood stopped what it was doing
to watch. Even those that weren't Muslims or even religious were proud
of this peaceful and incredibly powerful display of black manhood. It
symbolized a desire and a capability for black men to better. The men
at my Temple were invited and would've gladly participated in the his-
toric event but the march occurred on Yom Kippur, and if the Jewish
presence was been limited, their support was not. Yom Kippur means
"The Day of Atonement", and on that day, black Christians, Muslims
and Jews hoped for a new beginning. The already momentous day was
made even more special by the fact that my baby was so excited that she
kicked for the first time.

She was born in 1996 and that year in black Chicago the most popular baby names were those of luxury cars, brightly colored alcohol
beverages, but my baby got a good Hebrew name. I was always taught
that a name should be something that one should live up to and not
spend forever trying to live down. Her name is Emunah but we call her
Mooni for short. It means "faith", She was small and red and she never
cried and it frightened me for the first few days that after she was born,
I'd look at her and it was as if she weren't mine at all.

It was as if I was babysitting. I didn't feel for her what I thought a
mother should. I wasn't as over the moon as I thought I'd be. So many
teenage mothers find themselves in this very same predicament, and
without the proper education, support or spiritual understanding, they
get stuck, and this is where the cycle of neglect begins. It starts with an
emotional distance and escalates into worse. I've seen it in mothers
who thought the birth of the child would make the father stay. I had
seen what happens when a mother was never mothered herself, but

that wasn't me; I knew better. I had read about postpartum episodes, but I felt sure it would pass. I couldn't talk to anyone about it because I wasn't supposed to have had a baby anyway; people would've all said, "I knew she couldn't handle it," and I wouldn't give my family that kind of satisfaction. So I suffered. I thought to myself maybe I'm mad at her for making everybody hate me and ruining my life, but I quickly abandoned that idea. When people tried to blame my mother for my pregnancy, I took responsibility. It wasn't her fault and it certainly wasn't Mooni's. I prayed to God to help me get over it. When the baby was three days old my mother picked her up and said, "Hmm, she feels warm". I didn't know how warm or cold babies were supposed to be. My mother went and got a thermometer and Vaseline and proceeded to pull her pamper off. I was horrified; what was she doing? She saw the look on my face and said, "Sit down girl; this is how you take a baby's temperature." And with that she inserted the thermometer. I squealed, but it didn't hurt the baby at all. When my mother removed the thermometer, her voice changed from her normal one to a slightly more panicked one. She said, "Her temperature is 103. I'm gonna call the doctor". I sat there helpless, watching my mom be a mom. She called the emergency room and they told her that the baby should be brought in right away. I got the baby dressed and as I went to dress myself, my mother said, "No, you stay here. You have stitches and you can't come outside. The baby will be fine. I'll call you". With that, the door closed and I stood in the foyer alone, surrounded by baby stuff but no baby. I sat down on the couch and began to cry. Not only did I not have the faintest bond with this baby, she was sick and I didn't know how to take care of her.

A few minutes later someone came to the door. It was my aunt. My mother had called and told her what was going on and she didn't think I should be alone, so my aunt came over to sit with me. After she'd been there for about fifteen minutes, the phone rang. I could tell something was wrong by the way my aunt turned her back to me and lowered her head. When she turned back around, her eyes had begun to well up with tears and she said, "Sweetie the doctor wants to talk to you". My heart was nearly beating out of my chest. It seemed as if the world had stopped and I was about to be pushed off. The doctor asked me if I was the mother of the child and if I would authorize him to do a spinal tap. A spinal tap? What's that? As he explained, I couldn't hear him anymore. I sobbed and said okay, and it seemed as if before he had even finished talking my aunt and I were already in the car and on our way to the hospital. When we got there and walked in the door, the guards at the desk and the nurses that were standing around knew exactly who I was. One of the guard said, "That must be your pretty little girl back there, wrapped up in all those pretty blankets?" Yes, she was my baby. My pretty little girl and I didn't know what was wrong with her.

As we got closer to the room, I could hear her crying louder. In the room, my mother was holding her and they had put a little i.v. in her arm and I could see a little bit of blood around it and I my heart was breaking for her. Shots hurt adults, and she was only three days old. As I cradled her in my arms, trying my hardest to soothe her while needing to be soothed myself, the doctor walked in.

He put the x-rays on the viewer, and the images were of Mooni's brain. There was something on it that didn't belong. I began to scream. I couldn't bear to listen to what was going to come out of his mouth next. As far as I was concerned, there was nothing good that one could say when a newborn was sick and her brain was involved. I was so distraught that my mother and a nurse had to help me out of the room. At that moment I started to think that this was my punishment. I didn't want her, so God was going to take her back. A few hours before she had been a virtual stranger to me, but now I was on the floor begging God to let me keep her. She was mine, and I loved her. She was my baby and I didn't care about anything else.

The doctor told my mother that there was a blood clot on her brain and that when he performed the spinal tap, there was blood instead of spinal fluid. He also told her that Mooni might have meningitis. I knew what that was and I knew it was deadly. I have never been more afraid in my life. I sat there day and night. I slept there for thirteen days and the only time I put her down was when I had to visit the bathroom. I prayed for her. I prayed with more kavanah or intent, than I ever had. I chanted the sh'ma in my sleep. I begged for her life and I knew God heard me. One night, while sitting alone in the room with my baby, I felt God. I felt the same feeling that I did when I went back to Temple that day to see my friends. He was there and it was going to be okay. A few days later, the doctors told me that the blood clot had disappeared on its own. That's what the doctor said, but I had asked God to bring me closer to my daughter, and he did. After two weeks we finally went home, her healthy and me a mom.

I would take her to Temple and she would have a naming ceremony a few weeks later.

For the next couple of years she would be a "Temple Baby". That means from the time a mother walks through the doors of the Temple, her baby is everywhere, with everybody. While at Temple, the entire community takes part in looking after the children. I don't know that this is common at all synagogues, but it certainly seems popular amongst the black ones. She would have her first birthday party at Temple because all of our friends were there.

After Mooni was born, I became a more serious person. I wanted her to be surrounded by people who were like us. Being black and living in our neighborhood was going to teach her certain lessons, but those had to be balanced out with the ones she'd learn at Temple.

Two years later Iddo came along and that pregnancy had its own anxieties. Unlike with my daughter, this time I knew that I was having a boy. I was happy, sort of. He would be black, Jewish and male. All I could think of was how hard his life would be.

I still lived in Englewood and I was no stranger to the ills of the ghetto. I wondered how I was going to raise two children there and not lose them to poverty, gangs, or drugs. And once again, I leaned on God.

When I was five months pregnant and I learned I was carrying a boy, all the other anxieties took a back seat when I realized he would need to be circumcised. The anxiety that went with that made everything else seem trivial. For months, my son's brit gave me nightmares. I knew and understood why and even how, but how as a mother was I going to be able to allow someone to do that to my poor baby?

The pregnancy had been physically grueling, and its end was bittersweet. I knew that in just a few days my sweet little boy would have to go under the knife. The morning after he was born, the doctor asked if I'd like to have him circumcised, to which I answered, "Yes, but not today and not by you". The doctor had assumed that seeing "Jewish" noted in my records had to be a mistake. Not only did I not want my son circumcised at the hospital, I had already known for months the Mohel we would be using. The doctor didn't approve and I never saw him again.

The days leading up to the brit felt more like we were sitting Shiva than gearing up for a joyous occasion. The day finally came and if I hadn't been under the watchful eyes of so many, Iddo and I or "the boy" as he was affectionately called, would've headed for the border. It was awful. I apologized to him all day. I let him know it was nothing personal and that I didn't even really want to do it, but I had to. I was hoping that one day he would be able to forgive me for what I had to do. I had the wine and the bread and my mother prepared a meal and off to the Temple we went. My sons Brit would be the first performed in our actual Temple instead of in a home like usual. A Brit Milah is a big deal for Jews, it is the first time the new baby will be presented to the community and it is also the act of entering a son into the covenant between God and his creation. There were many people there in spite of the fact that it was a weekday and most of the attendees were the men in our congregation. I felt like the ancestors had come to welcome my son into the ages-old covenant. The men in attendance were members, and now my son was going to be. I was honored. I was still very nervous and very much afraid but the moment he left my hands and met the hands of my Abi, I was ok. The room was filled with my fathers and brothers, these *anshe chayil*, men of valor, and I knew my son was in good hands and one day he would grow to be just like these men. As much as I loved him and couldn't bear to see him in pain, neither could they. I was comforted by that thought.

After turning the baby over to the Godfather and hearing the Mohel so tenderly question my son, "Ha'im Atah *Ha Mashiach*, are you the Messiah?," a question that Jews have asked for thousands of years as we are still waiting for our Messiah to come. I retreated into the kitchen with some of the other women. First, I heard muffled voices, and then it became quiet. Then I heard my son begin to whimper, but the sound of his cry was drowned out by the loud cheers of *Mazel Tov*, followed by a chorus of a song that we sing called "Baruch Hashem". It was done; my son was now a full-fledged member of B'nai Yisrael, he had entered into the covenant of our ancestors.

From that day on, my son belonged to all the people that were in the room at the time of his Brit, and to the congregation. We all believed in the same God and the same law, black and white Jews, and the Mohel looked down at my beautiful black baby and acknowledged out loud for all to hear that, even he might possibly be the Messiah. You just had to be there.

CHAPTER 4

OLAM HABAH –
THE WORLD TO COME   עוֹלָם הַבָּא

Iwas a mom now, a real mom. I was a nose wiping, diaper changing, booboo kissing, double stroller toting, potty training, hair combing, tear wiping mom. I was concerned about things that I had been aware of before, but now I actually started to pay attention. I began to look at my children and other children and see their similarities and differences and I started very early on deciding which similarities I would allow to exist and which differences I would encourage. I wasn't certain of much, but I was positive that my children would be raised as Jews. Not in the way that I was raised as Jew, but better, more. I could speak and read Hebrew. I went to Temple every Shabbat, and I even sang in the choir and became a part of our women's group.

I was determined to immerse my children in this way of life, because I couldn't allow them to be immersed in the culture of our neighborhood. We lived in a place that was not far from my grandmother's house. It was a neighborhood that was and still remains one of the worst in the country. It was a place that I felt like I needed to escape from every day. It was poor and sad people. It was bad schools and drug houses. It was God forsaken, but even while living there, I knew I wasn't. I had escaped and come back.

I had lived for quite a while in a neighborhood that I believed was Shangri-la. It was one that was closer to the Jewish Day School which I had attended as a child. There was crime, but not as much as in other places. I could take leisurely walks at any time of day or night and I never feared violence. My curiosity had been satisfied I felt a great sense of gratification knowing I could survive anywhere.

However, when I moved back to Englewood from Hyde Park, things weren't quite as I remembered. Visiting friends in the neighborhood and actually living there were two totally different things. There were new faces and more vacant lots and board-ups. There was more crime because there were more drugs, and every time I watched the police or the feds make a bust, I cringed.

In principle, it was great to get the drugs off of the streets. The authorities were doing a good thing, what the taxpayers were paying them to do. But all I saw was trouble. A shortage of drugs to sell in my neighborhood meant that a war was coming. A war between those who had it to sell and those who didn't, while all of them depended on the income from it to feed their families. The fact that the supply was depleted never diminished the demand. This meant dealers killed dealers, sending many to the graveyard or jail. Some people resorted to robbery and burglary. This translated into more trouble for everyone in our neighborhood, even those who had jobs and worked every day.

I kept a hawkish eye on my children, as did my mother and my Uncle Larry, who had come to live with us. I had grown up being looked after by family, and so would my children. They would never go to daycare, but they would still learn. We would sit around the house and discuss everything: history, sports, the politics of the day, and the children would sit at their table coloring or eating or playing, but always listening and learning.

I can remember when my mother and I launched a massive family history project, the children went right along for the ride. I could take a two year old and a four year old to any library and they would play quietly. They may not have had a grasp of what we were doing, but they knew it was serious and in their own way they respected that. We traveled all over the country doing research. We talked to people that they didn't know. We went to nursing homes and did interviews with elderly family members, some of whom we had never met. We went to the plantation where our family worked as slaves and never once did the children behave like they didn't understand. It wasn't important to them, but I think they could see it was important to me and their grandma and they always behaved like I had a switch in my back pocket.

One day, my son, tucked underneath my uncle's left arm, shouted out after seeing President George Bush on the news, "George Bush is a sick Bastard!" He was three years old. I thought my uncle was going to whip his butt for cursing, but he found it hilarious. He replied to the boy's declaration with a great big grin and, "I Know that's right." My mother had a friend who came over regularly and she taught my son to call himself an "intellectual warrior". She was a teacher whom had taught African Studies for years. It seemed as if perhaps she had an added insight into what black males may have been missing and that's why she called him that. That's what he was and what they all have the potential of being.

My children may have lived in that neighborhood, but I was determined for that to not be their whole world. I spoke Hebrew to them around the house and we sang songs in Hebrew. By the time they were three, their little eyes could scour candy and cake wrappers for words like Gelatin, Animal fats, or Lard. They would always look for the kaph, the kosher K or the P for parve which meant it wasn't meat or dairy. They asked, "Is this kosher" when at birthday parties or eating at other people's houses. We went to Temple every Shabbat. We sang "Marching to Zion" when we were on our way to sleep, and, oh yes, they got proper home training. I knew that they had to have a balance, one that would help them navigate between worlds. I found this out the hard way and I was hoping to make it easier for them.

When summer came, we would sit on the porch and color or play or just talk, and the most amazing thing started to happen; they made friends. They were younger than most of the children that came over every single day to play with them, and they weren't allowed to leave the front of the house, and it seemed as if every child in the entire neighborhood found their way to our front porch, even on rainy days. I would sit out with them or in the living room window and watch and listen to them, and one day I can remember my son stomping into the house and informing me that he would be staying in the house for the rest of the day because, *"those* kids were out there cussin, and I don't wanna get a whuppin!" I found his toddler's outrage hilarious.

It was obvious my mother had learned from her mother. She was an awesome grandma. She was really great with the children. They loved her. She would sit out on the porch and read to them and tell them stories. She would buy them all ice cream and make them snacks. She would squash all of their quarrels and provide cotton balls, peroxide and band-aids to any scraped elbow or skinned knee in a one mile radius. She started a book club with them, and when she noticed the children that were having trouble reading or trouble at home, she always tried her best to help. Every year she hosted a block party with horses and clowns and jumping jacks and she would enlist the help of the entire block to buy school supplies for kids who didn't have any. All of the kids called her Grandma, and they all loved her.

My children were jealous sometimes, but she helped them understand. In some of their friends' homes, there weren't mothers or fathers; some lived with grandparents and some even with foster parents. Some of their parents were on drugs and they didn't have much, sometimes not even food. Some of them were drug babies, she explained that it made it harder for them to think, but them, they had a mommy and daddy and grandma and an uncle Jug where they lived. There were no drugs, violence or gangs. They had clothes, and food and they went a lot of places like the zoo, museums and took trips all the time. Because my kids were so blessed, they had to learn to share their blessings with others, and their friends liked to come to our house to feel just for a little while the way my kids got to feel all the time: safe.

I knew my daughter had learned compassion when she would came to me and asked if one of her friends from the block could go to Arkansas with us for our family reunion because, "I don't want to leave her here by herself. She never gets to go anywhere". I knew what tzedakah, charity was, and my mother had taught them. It was around this same time that my mother decided to run for office. I believe she was inspired to do so by all of the "grandchildren" that sat on her porch each day. Her opponent had more money to spend on the campaign and my mother lost, but it was okay because it was another possibility that my mother showed the neighborhood children. They made signs and were proud to say they knew her when they walked through the neighborhood and saw her name in people's windows and front yards. Most of all, my children were learning how the political process worked and the importance of their vote and their voice, and how there was always a way that they could change things. My daughter was nearly the same age I had been when I helped get the vote out for Mayor Washington or just plain old "Harold" as he was affectionately called.

My children never did go to any daycare or preschool, even though the school that all of the kids on my porch went to was on the corner of our block. A public school education would not give them the quality of education I had received, and I felt the best thing was to apply the lessons from my past to my children's future. That is how I made the decision of sending my children to, of all places, Jewish day school, the same one I had attended as a child.

We were Jews. That's who we were, so in my mind there was no better place for my children than Jewish school. I couldn't trust the education of my children to anyone else. I had had problems at the school, but as a mother I saw the value in what they offered. I knew that without my Jewish education I would've been a much different person, someone I wouldn't have been as proud of. What I had learned there far outweighed what I didn't learn. I learned most of the customs of Ashkenazi Jews at the school, and what I couldn't learn there about being a Jew, I learned at Temple. I learned to speak Hebrew and D'aaven, pray and read Torah. I learned to read the writing of the Jewish sage, Rashi, and how to speak a little Russian and Yiddish from my friends. I was better at Math, Science, History and English than the majority of the rest of the kids when I got to public school. I went to school every day with people who didn't look like me and lived around people who did, so I learned to never feel out of my element. I didn't know it at that time, but I had the best of both worlds.

I had gone to a different school before going to my Jewish school, one at which Santa Claus came around Christmas, and the Easter bunny came in the spring and I didn't want my children exposed to that. I had wrestled with feelings of isolation and jealousy when all of the rest of the children were getting presents from Santa, and when I said he wasn't real, I lost friends. I wanted to be happy and enjoy these treats just like them, but I couldn't because I was a Jew, and that's not what we did. I didn't want my children to have to deal with that kind of confusion; life was already challenging enough.

I couldn't imagine what my life would've been like had I not had all of the Jewish teachings that I did. I can remember what a huge disappointment it was for me when I got to my all-black public school and realized that it wasn't a factory for black revolutionaries and intellectuals. I had learned that I couldn't count on any school to teach the entire truth, and I taught this to my children. I was unconcerned about what people in my neighborhood or anywhere else would think, putting my children in an all-black school wouldn't serve them the best socially, educationally, or spiritually. They were always black, all the time, everywhere they went, and I didn't believe they would forget that if they went to Jewish school. Conversely, no one would look at them and say, "They must be Jewish" they didn't look like most Jews, but they were, and I wanted them to be reminded of that as much as they were reminded of their being black. I wanted them to learn just as much about their Jewish identity as their black one and to be just as comfortable with it. I knew I hadn't gotten what I'd hoped I would out of going to public school, but I did get what my mother and my uncle had hoped I'd get out of Hebrew school. The choice was clear.

When black people found out I was Jewish, they would sometimes accuse me of being confused or trying to be white, or they would try to shame me by informing me that the Jews killed Jesus. As a child, I didn't know what to say or feel about these situations. As an adult, I knew my faith was the most important thing in the world to me. My life revolved around it. I can remember overhearing the children on the porch talking about the police and what happens when you go to jail, and after listening for a minute, my heart sank. These children, not much more than babies, had an eerily accurate idea of what the criminal justice system was like, all the way down to "good time" and putting something on someone's "books". It was crazy and the worst part was that God never came up once. The police and judges were the law in the world they were living in and nothing was higher. I couldn't let that be the understanding that my children would have.

I needed my children to fear God, especially my son. I had attended a school with mostly white kids in an upper middle class neighborhood, and I had tried to escape, ignore and detach myself from the neighborhood that I was from, but I never could. I saw what my neighborhood could and would do to a black man. As a young teenager, I saw boys younger than me standing on the corner yelling, "one time" whenever the police drove down the street to alert boys only a little older than me to hide the crack they were selling. I lay on the floor during gun battles between the Folks on my side of the boulevard and the Black Stones on the other.

I had a cousin who was not much more than a baby himself when he became one of the most feared gamblers in our neighborhood. He would come home sometimes with entire paychecks won from grown men. He reminded me of the character "C" from the movie *Bronx Tale*. He would go to jail on and off for this over the years and his addiction to luck and money would later lead him into other, more dangerous, lines of work, but I don't believe that was ever really him. I think sometimes parents in the ghetto unwittingly prepare our children only to survive in the ghetto or in jail. We don't prepare them for the type of life we want them to have; instead, we prepare them for the one that they have at the moment. If we don't prepare them for better things, they'll never know that it's okay to want something better, and I think that's what happened with my cousin. He got trapped on the other side as so many good kids do. Perhaps it was easier for my mother, she had two girls, than it was for my aunt, who had a boy. There is an immense amount of fear and anxiety that comes with having a black son. Every moment from the time he draws breath you worry about him because there are so many things that he will have to fight against. He will have to fight other people, racism, his own people and even sometimes himself. Black mothers were "Tiger Moms" long before there was a term to describe us. We had to go hard on our girls, and extra hard on our boys because we had to keep them in their place or "Massa" would sell them off. We had to make them strong and weak at the same time. We had to teach them what they could say, when they could say it and how, to whom, and where. We had to save them from themselves. This has left a lasting scar on the African American community, and to this day we haven't recovered from having our roles scripted and twisted by the world both inside and outside the black community. It was, and still is, awful. Yet, it has to be done to save them from the streets, the penitentiary, and each other.

I cringe as every black mother does when we hear of the straight A star athlete and all-around good boy being gunned down. We think about all of these things and they scare the hell out of us. So what do we do? We discipline them. We whip them, we tell them not to cry, we tell them to man up, but how in the world does a four year old do that? I understood this technique because it was the one that was employed to make the boys in my family into men, but I also saw the error in it. My aunts and uncles didn't rear the boys in our family that way because they hated them or wanted them to be trapped in the cycle of violence and poverty in the neighborhood. They believed that it was the only way to save them, but it also made it harder for them. I whipped my children, both of them, but only when they needed it. I didn't mind them crying because that was the point of a whipping anyway. How do I know you got the point if you don't cry? I wanted them to learn to equate doing bad things with pain. I didn't believe in time outs, toy deprivation or any of that new school parent crap. I was old school with one exception; I didn't mind explaining to my children why they were getting a whipping to help them understand. In the end, it always boiled down to "mommy, I'm sorry. I know I shouldn't have did that," and it was over. I also believed in praising them when they did something right. I believed in being a kid with them once in a while and kissing them until my lips got chapped. I let them see me cry when I was hurt, just as I let them see me laugh when I was happy. I let them see that I was human just like them, and the same way I could hurt them, they could hurt me. They saw I cared about their feelings and they cared about mine. I didn't want my son to be a man; I wanted him to be a four year old. I didn't want him to learn not to cry; I wanted him to cry because I wanted him to learn that there were consequences for his actions and that people cry when they are hurt.

I had seen children that went undisciplined and have seen the thoughts on the faces of so many black women in the grocery store or on the bus when they see a child acting a fool. I could look at the horror and disgust on each of their faces and silently utter in unison right along with them, "No, Lawd, couldn't be mine actin like that". We understand that unruly black children aren't cut the same slack that unruly children of other ethnicities are. Some children that go undisciplined are called spirited or strong-willed, black children are called bad. Some children that go undisciplined grow up to be called, CEO, Senator, or maybe even Mr. President, but some black children grow up to be called inmate number 123456. It's not fair, but whether we like it or not, it is what it is. I knew raising my son with my values in the hood might earn him the label of being soft, but I didn't plan for him to stay in the hood, so it didn't matter what the neighborhood had to say. Just as I didn't live for the hood to validate me, neither would my children. I wanted them to be looked at as different, especially my boy.

When my daughter was five, it was time for her to go to school and for me it was like going to school for the first time all over again. However, there was a whole lot more anxiety. She was supposed to start school September 12, 2001, but the school was closed, just like everything else because of the attack on the World Trade Center which had occurred just the day before.

I had no idea how much preparation went into enrolling a kid in school, but it took even more with this school because there was money involved, lots and lots of it. I started the process of enrolling my daughter in late July, even though I had known for months that I intended for her to go there. The day I went to pick up her paperwork, I felt relieved when I saw a few of the old faces there. The principal was the same, a few of my old teachers were there, and even my grandmother's old friend was there. She was still the school secretary, but she had been elevated to the role of "school matriarch". I was so happy to see her. I sat and chatted with her until the new person who was head of the kindergarten and preschool called me into her office. We talked about the program briefly and then we walked around a bit and finally we got to the first classroom my daughter would ever be in, my own kindergarten room.

The oven that my friends and I used to take turns trying to stuff each other into was still there. The reading corner was still there, though the pillows had been changed, and the toilets were smaller than I remembered. All in all it was still very much the way I remembered it and I felt much better. As I left the building, I was handed the packet with the medical forms, emergency forms, handbook and tuition charges. The school cost an arm a leg and at least three fingers off of the hand that was still attached to my remaining arm. It was nuts. The price of the tuition in Jewish day school was double and in some cases, triple, the amount of other parochial schools in our neighborhood. I had to ask my mother how she had afforded it. As a child I knew it had been a struggle for her, but as an adult I finally understood it. She told me how she had had to work all the time to afford the tuition and when she couldn't pay, my uncle did. She also told me that she had wanted to move away from her mother's house much sooner than we did ,but she knew if we had, she wouldn't have been able to afford for us to live somewhere nice and still afford for me go to that school. If we had moved, I would have had to go to a neighborhood school and my education was too important for that. She wasn't preparing me for the world that I lived in at that time, but for the one she wanted me to live in. My mother helped me put it all into perspective and I knew what I had to do. School started a few weeks later, in September, but my daughter didn't start for a week and a half after the rest of the children because that is how long it took for us to come up with the tuition.

The experience of being a mom of a child attending Jewish day school was much different from a child attending Jewish day school. When I saw all of the old face that were so instrumental in shaping so many of my thoughts and ideas, I felt secure that my children would be receiving the same quality of education that I did. I was soon to learn that the faces I had known before were about the only thing that I would recognize.

CHAPTER 5

IF I MAKE
MY BED IN HELL

וְאַצִּיעָה שְׁאוֹל הִנֶּךָּ

The night before Mooni's first day of school, I hardly slept at all. I lay there staring at the pictures taped to my mirror and then at the ceiling, then the wall, and back to the photos on the mirror. My girl was in most of the pictures; some were from special occasions, others just hanging around the house. In the pictures, she looked like such a baby, but she wasn't. She was a big girl who would be going to school the next day. She was so excited about her first day. We had picked out a pair of Levi's with little purple flowers on the back pockets and a purple chenille sweater with a pair of lilac Mary Janes. Her ensemble was topped off by braided hair adorned with silver and white beads. Venus and Serena didn't have nothing on her. She had had her backpack all ready to go for at least three weeks, but was unable to use it because it took us so long to come up with her tuition.

The more I thought about it the worse I felt. She was going in nearly three weeks late; I didn't want her to feel the awkwardness of being the only kid in the class who didn't know what was going on. She asked me every day, am I going to school today? I didn't know how to tell her that it was my fault she wasn't there and that I was a loser. It was awful. I didn't want her to feel bad or self conscious like I was feeling then and then I realized she would be fine, but I still wasn't.

The next morning we got in the car and before turning the corner of our block, tears had already began to well up in my eyes. The girl who I prayed that I'd just get through the first day with was now a five year old with a book bag and a lunch box and was on her way to school. As we walked to the door, my heart began to pound. I knew in a few minutes I'd leave my baby here alone for the first time, like my mother once did. Would she cry for me like I did for my mom? Maybe it was shame; all of the other parents had started their children on time. What would they say about me, what would they think of me? I was still a little intimidated by the old faces at the school; they still made me feel like a child.

As we stepped in the door, the pounding in my chest got so loud that I could barely hear the sound of our steps. I turned to walk into the office where I was to deliver the check, but I was stopped by my grandmothers old friend yelling, She's late, take her to class!. So, once again, I would make that walk, but this time I was the escort. All of the same smells were present: school glue, popcorn, and play dough. As we walked up the stairs, I held her little hand tighter, not ever wanting to let go, but in that instant, in the silence of that same hallway I heard it: the theme music, shhhh,shhhh,shhhh, the same sound that her hair beads was making, my braided hair had made twenty years before. Her steps made her hair sway back and forth and the sound jarred me into the realization that the last time I heard that sound I was a daughter, and today I was a mother. I let go of her little hand as it hit me; somewhere in all of this I had grown up and I had to let her grow up too. As I let her hand go, I could feel the tears welling up once again; this time one even slid down my cheek. I knocked on the door and with a deep breath turned the knob and walked in. It all looked so familiar. Her teacher walked over to us and smiled warmly and as she began rubbing my shoulder in consolation, she stuck out her hand to my daughter and she shook it. She said, Tell mom that you re going to be fine and you re gonna have fun. Before she could get the words out, Mooni was swarmed by a group of kids, all marveling at her beaded hair. It was like déjà vu. She was gone. Instantly popular, she was now officially a kindergartner.

I talked to her teacher for a few more minutes and it turns out she was also an excellent therapist, so within about ten minutes I was calm enough to leave my baby. As I turned to leave, I called out my daughter's name. When she looked around, I feebly waved and put on my brave face. She stopped what she was doing and came over and gave me a big hug. She said, "Mommy, I'll be okay and you can come back and get me when today is over. I'll be waiting for you right here", she pointed. I was never that well adjusted or brave. I walked out the door fighting back the tears yet once again. She was such a big girl, and she seemed even bigger than me.

As I walked through the hall and back down the stairs, the familiar feeling of loathing and discomfort set in once again. I had to go into the office and do adult business. I felt like I was ten years old all over again. I sat in the waiting area until I was called into the principal's office where she and someone else who also had an official role at the school but who I didn't know sat. For the next thirty minutes, we would politely discuss if my daughter's attendance at the school would be too much of a financial burden for my family. I felt so poor and small and much the way my mother must've felt the times she swallowed her pride for me. I said what I had to say in a way that they found satisfactory and then it was time for me to leave. I didn't like it, but I knew it was the best thing for my child. Perhaps all that happened between me and the school wasn't water under the bridge as I had previously thought, but that too was fine as long as we could all pretend that it was.

School let out at 3:30, I was back in the parking lot by 2:00. I would've been there earlier but I didn't want to look like the obsessed, separation-anxiety-suffering parent that I was. After I had been there for a few minutes, I saw her. Her class had come out for recess and she was right in the thick of things. She was on the jungle gym, then the slide and next the sandbox. It made me giggle when while in the sandbox the wind blew and she instantly jumped up and checked her hair, brushing it with her hand making sure there was not one particle of sand in it. She continued to play with her new friends and she played so hard she didn't even know I was there. I felt so much better knowing that all of the things that had kept me up that previous night had proven to be nothing more than a case of the jitters. She was fine and looking at her, you couldn't even tell it was her first day.

School was finally over and just as she said, she was waiting for me. She was happy and that made me happy, and all of the anxiety that I had felt that day melted away. Her face lit up when she saw me, and she ran over, jumping and bouncing. She had so many things to tell me that just started spilling out so fast that it sounded like gibberish and it made me laugh. She was so excited. As we turned to walk away, her teacher called out to me and we stopped. She came over and said, "Today Emunah did the cutest thing. When she got up to introduce herself to the class, she made up a little song for her name!" I was embarrassed; I knew exactly what the song was because I had taught it to her, and I had learned it from Jay-Z. It was a song called "Izzo," and instead of singing those letters, her name went perfectly with the beat, E to the M U N to the AH ! It was great.

We got in the car and as soon as we were all buckled in, I would ask her the question that I've asked her every single day since that on: How was school? Start from the time I dropped you off. She went on and on, and I loved to see her so excited about school. It didn't matter what deals I had had to cut or how bad of a beating my ego took; it was all worth it. To see her happy made all of the other stuff seem small.

Over the course of the year, I became a fixture in the classroom. I wanted to do all of the things with my daughter that my mother could never do because she was always working. I was there for every class trip from the zoo to the apple orchard, and I always brought her brother along. I was there for swimming classes and even there for her hundred day celebration. It made me feel good to be able to be there for her, but each day I dreaded talking about money, which seemed to come up more than I cared for it to.

That first year at the school I paid close attention to the affect that the school and the children in it were certain to have on my daughter. Her classroom was a loving environment, her teachers made it that way, and the all of the kids were nice. It was one of inclusion and all of the kids and even the teachers marveled at her newest hairstyle or what funny things she would say. They loved her because she was considerate of other people's feelings and she was smart. Her sweet disposition, along with her

manners made her the most sought-after play date in the entire kindergarten. She had black friends, white friends and one Asian friend whose name was often mangled, much to her chagrin, by her little brother, who called him "yucky monster."

Her classroom looked much like mine did when I was in kindergarten except there were a few more Jews who were Orthodox, but other than that it was almost the same. At the end of the year I felt satisfied with the choice that I had made. I could see it in the way that she spoke sometimes and the things she spoke about, even the way that she played had changed. But the change wasn't enough to keep the neighborhood kids off of our porch.

One day while I was out running errands near the school, I saw the parent of one of my daughter's classmates, the parent of the only other black kid in the class. We stopped and talked for a moment and what she said shocked me. She told me that her daughter, who had been one of my daughter's closest playmates, wasn't going to be coming back to the school in the fall. She was going to a neighborhood Catholic School. When I asked why, she informed me that my Jewish day school didn't allow non-Jews past kindergarten. When I was there, no such rule existed. There had been children in my class of all different religious backgrounds and it wasn't a problem. I always thought it was up to parents to figure out what was best for their children to learn. I understood that if one sent their Christian or Muslim child to a Jewish school, they would no more become Jews than a black kid in an all white school became white. Sure, they might learn about Judaism, but that wouldn't make them Jews. I didn't like it and I didn't understand it, but I knew that my daughter wouldn't be alone; she had other friends there. I was certain in the fall there would be new kids enrolling who would provide the same diversity that I had seen in my own classroom.

Summer drew to a close and it was time to do the tuition dance again. It was gut wrenching. I will never forget the first day; we saw a few of her friends from kindergarten, but not as many as I'd hoped. The ones who bought diversity to the class were no longer there, and after closer examination I saw there was no diversity anywhere except the diversity that was holding my hand. My daughter was the only non-white in the whole school with the exception of a bi-racial kid a grade above her. I was bothered by this, but it seemed that she wasn't, so I didn't say anything. She was happy because it was her school and she knew all of the people and she had friends, but it was clear to me this was definitely not my school anymore.

In first grade my daughter really started to learn Hebrew. She learned the sounds of the letters and simple words and how to count. She started learning a little bit about Torah, and just as my Uncle had talked to me, I talked to her. She was always so impressed that I knew what she was doing and I understood what she was saying. She inspired me to want to learn more and want to get back to my studies. I wanted to get better because she was getting better and I wanted to be able to understand what she was doing. I wanted to know everything that she was being taught, the same way my uncle did. We discussed her lessons every day and I did my best to balance them.

Near the beginning of the year, my rabbi announced that after the Holy Days that year, he would begin counting women in a minyan, a Jewish quorum consisting of 10 men, and calling us to Torah on a regular basis. I was the first to volunteer and he was criticized for including me, but he paid it no attention. Ours would be the only black Jewish Temple in the country that would allow women to be included in every facet of the service. I was always good at reading Torah, but I was a girl so, it didn't matter. Until then, there weren't many options for those of us at Temple who wanted to contribute but couldn't cook.

I had always had a knack for the language. I could read and D'aaven or pray very well, but never had an opportunity to showcase my talent. It was an honor to be able to be called to the Torah when it wasn't my Baht Mitzvah. I wanted Mooni to see that women were equal to men, and that my skill was just as valued and respected as theirs.

As the years went by, I still visited the school, though not as much as I had when my daughter was in kindergarten. I was curious about the way the changing ethnic mix of the students would influence the curriculum. I loved that my daughter was receiving a Jewish education; I only wished she weren't the only black student at school. Still, Mooni seemed perfectly comfortable at school, and I never suggested that there might be anything to be concerned about. At one time, I had naively believed that we were all Jews and we were all the same, but my experiences had taught me a different lesson.

I didn't go there with the hopes of being right or my fears being realized. I wanted to be wrong but in an environment like this one it was impossible for me to be. People have prejudices. The problem is that most don't recognize the prejudices they have until they are confronted with them, and maybe not even then. If you don't live around prejudice, work with it, encounter it at the supermarket, you have no real mechanism to understand prejudices when confronted with them. This is Chicago, and there are reasons why most of us choose to live where we do. We have long been the most segregated city in the country and we remain that way. Every group in the city is implicated and impacted by this segregation even Jews and blacks. I knew this and I saw evidence of it every day, but my daughter was flourishing and that was enough. I was just there to make sure no one tried to change her name.

Most of the people at the school were Jews, but they were different. Yes, they would really probably get a laugh out of me calling *them* different, but they were. I was familiar with Jews of all kinds, especially the ones who were most friendly. I wasn't uncomfortable with my daughter being around whites, but I was uncomfortable that many of the Jews in her school weren't as friendly as those at my Temple or other places we visited. I knew these people; they were the ones who would look at me like I was lost when I went into their neighborhoods or to shop in their stores. They were Orthodox Jews. They wore long black coats and big black hats, black pants and black shoes with a white shirt and long curly side burns with large bushy beards. They were all white, however, I have of late heard talk of a few black Orthodox Jews. Their women wore long skirts and kept their heads covered, with a kerchief or a wig. Other Jews didn't distinguish themselves this way. The Orthodox had created a uniform that would set them apart.

While our interaction was intentionally limited, I'm sure, over the years, now I saw them every day. It was clear to me that these were the Jews that were most bothered by my daughter's presence in the school. Some Orthodox considered themselves quite liberal for even allowing their boys to sit in a classroom with a girl, but a "shvartz" was something totally different. If Mooni had been mentally challenged or had some other deficit besides the color of her skin, she could've been explained away as a charity case; all Jews are encouraged to do good deeds, especially those that deal with doing charity for the poor and underprivileged.

Mooni may have been poor and even underprivileged, but she was smart, too smart for pity or sympathy. She was the intellectual equal of any of the children in her class, and this in itself was contrary to what most of their parents believed. She was not a comrade; she was a competitor, and the worst kind: one that might show the other children up, despite being black. I believe this created a conflict of conscience within the school's entire Orthodox community. Her very presence in the school sent curious children asking questions of their parents that parents never wanted to hear. They were no longer competing with children that looked like them; this was something else. To place second in such a competition said more to them about the Orthodox community than it did about any one child.

While there was no racial diversity at Mooni's school, I had found some measure of comfort in the religious diversity at first. There were the conservative and reform mothers who drove their minivans with two car seats in the back and the ski rack on top. Then there were the mothers who stood around in a circle, hovering over their jogging strollers, chatting and zipping through their blackberrys to arrange play dates. There were the nannies, au pairs, companions and babysitters who were for the most part foreign blacks. This was the group I was most commonly mistaken to belong to.

One day I was asked which child was I the companion of? After realizing what I was actually being asked, I very nicely turned to the woman who asked and informed her that I hadn't been the companion of a kid since I was a kid myself. After discovering that the child I picked up every day was my own, neither she nor any of the other nannies ever spoke to me again. I am sure that somewhere the mothers who wore the long skirts and kerchiefs or wigs stood around and did something, but they definitely didn't do it around the rest of us because all of their kids were bussed in. I didn't fit in really anywhere, but my daughter did. I became friendly with the mothers of Mooni's friends. We talked about play dates and vacation plans just as the other parents did, but unlike their relationships with the other parents, that was the extent of our involvement. I didn't go to extracurricular school functions and I didn't hang out with them in my free time, but that was okay as long as my daughter was happy.

During this time I became more involved with the activities of the children at my Temple. I figured that perhaps they could learn along with my daughter via her hand outs, coloring sheets and activity pages from school. I really wanted them to have a greater understanding of who they were and to be able to articulate to their friends in the non-Jewish world that Jews were different in more ways than just going to "church on Saturday" and avoiding pork. I had struggled with my Jewish identity when I attended public school, and I could only imagine how much worse it would've been had I only attended public school. Being raised a Jew in a home where many parents don't speak Hebrew and attending a school where religion or identity is never even discussed, and Temple on Shabbat is the only time and place you hear the language and learn Jewish history can be hard and confusing for a child. I sought to alleviate some of that.

My daughter had Jewish friends and I admired the way that they interacted with one another. Their conversations about their homes and what they did and didn't do there, about their Temples and their lives as Jews, were natural and easy. It became so easy that Mooni and her friends would begin to speak to each other in Hebrew like it was their own secret language. It was then that I began to notice that when Mooni was around her friends at Temple, she started to be less relaxed. The more she learned at school, the less she wanted the other children at Temple to know. She was ashamed that she knew the words to the prayers and understood the service in a way that the other kids may not have. I may have pressured her a bit too much to be a good student, but I just wanted her to do better than I had. She didn't want to be miss goody goody at Temple. She just wanted to be like all of the rest of the kids. I hated that, but I understood it. I had hoped that getting the other kids more involved would help her get past her embarrassment.

The children from Temple, Mooni and I, started doing things together, hanging out, taking fieldtrips and doing special projects. I believe it was good for all of us. Before long, we were our own little group and shortly thereafter started to receive invites to be a part of things that involved other Jewish and teen groups from all over the city.

I had only rarely interacted with the Ashkenazim (descendants of European Jews), so organizing activities for the two groups was new for me. I had talked to them at school about simple issues involving our children or dealt with them only when they'd come and visit our Temple, but I had never really worked with them and perhaps that was a bit of my own prejudice. The more our projects and relationships progressed; I realized that many of the adults that I was working with were the same kids I had gone to Jewish day school with, just all grown up. It wasn't that I didn't know how to work with them or that I was afraid to, I think bias and life's hard knocks over the years had caused me to forget. I had made the mistake of lumping all Ashkenazi Jews together, just as so many people do black folk. They had differences–we all had differences–but what was important was that I finally remembered, we also had similarities.

I was working not only with Jewish organizations, but interdenominational ones too, and if some of the children in Ashkenazi groups had learned that all Muslims were bad, their opinions were quickly changed after working together on projects that would benefit communities that neither of them came from nor lived in; the children and parents saw only people who needed help, and help they did. They served together in the service of others because both Jewish and Muslim doctrine emphasizes the importance of charity and social justice.

Whereas their faiths had once kept them apart, it was now bringing them together. There were events where the children would get together and discuss texts from the Bible, Torah and Qu'aran regarding treatment of others and charity and social ethics and responsibility. They would do this while wearing jeans and t –shirts, hijabs and baseball caps, eating pizza and drinking sodas: just being kids. They all contributed to the conversation. They talked about their experiences in their neighborhoods and their schools, and how their faith was a factor there or not. They talked about their problems and tried to help each other find solutions, and I just thought it was wonderful. They were all from different churches, mosques and temples, but when they were together they were all the same.

At our Temple we were Jews, but in our meetings there were Jews that weren't just like us either. Sure, all Jews didn't believe in all of the same things as Christians and Muslims, but our similarities when we worked together were magnified. There were Reform, Reconstructionist and Conservative Jews, and then there was us, the Black Jews. I was proud to see the others standing with me in the name of all that was good, and they too were proud to have me there. Not once did someone not being religious enough or kosher enough or the color of my skin or theirs come up. It didn't matter. We were Jews and all there to serve a purpose greater than any of the petty reasons that Jews often find to divide the faith. We were there to help ourselves, help the people in our communities, and ideally help the world. I couldn't help but wonder why there was not an Orthodox kid in the bunch. This was good and spiritually edifying work that we were doing; it was what the Torah teaches that we should do. So why wouldn't the ultra-religious want to be involved?

Our differences as Jews were becoming more and more obvious to me. I had been under the impression that all Ashkenazi Jews were essentially the same, but once again I had been proven wrong. It wasn't the first time, and it wouldn't be the last. Despite being a minority amongst minorities—a black Jew—I continued to confront and grapple with my own biases. Though I was facing my own prejudices, I couldn't help but notice that in these honorable organizations and at all of the interfaith events we attended, there were always a group of Jews who were absent. The Orthodox wanted no part of us or diversity.

We were never invited into their neighborhoods, and they never came into ours, and until I started working with other Jews that were not black, I thought we had been shunned by all white Jews. This was very interesting to me and I began to pay closer attention to the pattern that emerged. I studied it in the news, on the streets and at our Temple, but most importantly I started to study it much closer at my daughters' school. It was most apparent there.

I watched the Reform and Conservative parents speak in hushed tones when the Orthodox would come around. The Reform, Conservative and other Jewish movements were more liberal and Americanized than their European counterparts. I began to think the Orthodox were the Jews that many other Jews subconsciously wanted to be, that they felt some shame at not being as committed to the faith. The other parents would whisper when they would admit to other parents that they didn't keep kosher or only kept kosher to a certain degree, or quietly admitted that they drove on the Sabbath.

The Orthodox were the picture of piety, but not to me. I didn't have a concept of who they even were until I was a teenager, and even then I didn't really understand. At that point, all Ashkenazi Jews were the same to me and I was under the impression that they all saw me as the same. When I saw firsthand that the Ashkenazi Jews that lived in more integrated areas were much different from those who lived in the more segregated Jewish enclaves of the North Side, I realized I had been unfair. I can't say that those who shared the same neighborhood as other races and ethnicities weren't prejudiced at all; however, I can say if they were, they were hiding it better than most. I believe it was because the Jews in more integrated neighborhoods knew how to interact with people of other races because they saw them every day, but on the North Side the coping mechanism of choice is simply to ignore what doesn't look like you and pray they don't force you to engage them.

I had no impulse to be close friends with the Orthodox at all; they represented the religion of many of the grandparents of the other parents at the school, but they didn't represent mine. I had never been taught to fear or revere them, but others had. In the minds of some, they were the gold standard of Judaism. It was a club that so many wanted to get into, but they just couldn't stop eating cheeseburgers, driving on Shabbat or wearing pants, and for this they were shunned, belittled and judged. I felt so sorry for them. I was black, which granted me a kind of immunity to this madness, and that worked out great because I didn't like being bullied. I knew how much they abhorred me and how they viewed my daughter, but it didn't scare me; it only ticked me off.

After overhearing conversations between angry parents and embarrassed children being chastised for allowing "that girl" to succeed where their child, and God forbid, their male child, had failed, and intense dialogue coming to an abrupt end when I walked into the room, something told me Mooni was supposed to be there.

After that I once again become a student. I approached the new situation in a much different way than I had before. I knew that God had called me to send my children to this school. However, just because I believed didn't mean it wasn't going to be a fight. There were a lot of arguments.

There were arguments with my family about what was best for them. Then there was the fight with their dad's family whom I had once gone to for help with tuition payments but they said no. They were not Jews. They went to church and could not understand the importance of a Jewish education nor see its benefits. I once had a college professor assign me the task of writing a paper on why I, a Black Nationalist, would send my jet black children to a lily white school. I had to defend my decision to many a black parent and even some non-parents who championed public schools and advised me that my children would be better served there. Why, I was asked over and over again, would you want to leave them in an environment like that? To which Stevie Wonder taught me to answer, "God knew exactly where he wanted them to be placed".

I knew that this wasn't about academics, religion or even race. It was about my children's true identities and how they should go about finding it. I had been sidetracked so many times in my search for my own that I would not allow my children those distractions. I knew that they wouldn't find spirituality at school, but they would experience resistance, and through that, they would see real Judaism and what it really meant to them when they had to defend theirs. I knew that they wouldn't be presented with a complete view of Hebrew culture, history and language in our Temple because many of us were still learning those things, while some of us weren't into learning them at all. I knew that they wouldn't learn to be black in a public school because I surely didn't, just as I had learned it at home, I taught it there also. I was on my own. My children were in a place that no one but me wanted them to be, but that didn't matter to me because I believed it would ultimately make them better people, and better Jews.

Iddo entered the school when Mooni was in second grade. He was in kindergarten and he had a much different take on the place than his sister did. He didn't like it, not at all. A few days after starting school and observing his new classmates and surroundings, he arrived at a fascinating conclusion: kindergartners play too much and they all talk back to the teacher and everybody needed a whuppin!

He was annoyed by most of the other children. These kids were different, and the school he had just started was nothing like the neighborhood we lived in. On our block, he was used to playing football and baseball and cops and robbers. He didn't even understand the concept of a sandbox or duck, duck, goose. Who is there to beat in duck, duck, goose; what kind of man plays that game anyway? He was a five-year-old boy, not a man, and he didn't know how to play like other five-year-olds or even understand the point of it.

For the first month or so, his teachers were under the impression that he couldn't talk because he wouldn't talk to them. However, he told me everything, down to the most insignificant of details of his day, every day. When I talked to the teachers, they were in awe. Who even knew the boy was paying attention? I realized that the school was a bit of a shock for him because he wasn't like his sister. He wasn't warm and outgoing; he was serious and a little introverted. He was opinionated and always well-behaved, but the biggest difference was he was a black male and I never forgot that or the way that the world viewed him. I watched him closely and what I began to see in him, set off a torrent of different emotions inside of me. I realized that despite all of my efforts, my son was already being conditioned to survive in the hood, and nowhere else.

He couldn't relate to children who were always happy and engaged in childish fun. If he wasn't beating someone or locking somebody up or getting away from the police, it wasn't fun, and even worse, pointless. He was already learning how to survive in the world of the ghetto, but not in the world that I so badly wanted for him. He had learned through playing with his friends on the block that if he wasn't the most dominant and the fastest and strongest, then he was a punk. They never once factored in how smart he was or how smart they were because it was never really about that. It was about who you could beat and how badly. It was the law of the jungle, and he was only five. It really hit me one day we were driving to school and the police pulled alongside of me as I sang along with the radio. My son immediately went into panic mode. He was worried that the police were going to pull me over and take me to jail because that's what happened in the games he and his friends played and that's what the other children had told him happened to their parents or people they knew. I asked him, what is a cop's job? All he could say was, "to lock people up". Not once did he say anything about protecting good people from the bad guys.

I acted upon Iddo s aversion to childish games by encouraging his tolerance for less serious play, but I felt sad that kids growing up in our neighborhood had no idea how to be kids, and I wondered what kind of adults they would become if they got that far. As time went on, he became more tolerant and began to enjoy the games that children at school played and enjoyed less those of his friends on our block. He began to enjoy the life of a stress-free six-year-old. He didn't mind an occasional romp in the sandbox or finger painting or even making mother's day gifts out of pipe cleaners and tissue paper rolls. He had turned into regular kid, no longer a mini man with the weight of the world on his shoulders.

He was in this new place along with his sister and I was always there with them. There was no other place for me. I knew what they were up against. The arguments of some of the dissenters like they would be mistreated or singled out and punished, were valid and I had my own misgivings, so I was vigilant. Every day, my children and I had a routine. On the drive home they would tell me everything that had happened during their day. I wanted to hear everything. I also wanted them to learn how to tell a story from beginning to end and learn to articulate their feelings, but most importantly, I wanted them to know how much I cared about what they had to say. They would often fight over who would go first, so we had to work out a system of alternating days. I was happy that they enjoyed sharing with me as much as they did. I heard other parents speak of how their children never told them anything, while I couldn't shut mine up.

One day, Mooni, who was a real social butterfly, showed me that she had become a pro at navigating her worlds. She knew who she was in both places and it didn't confuse her at all. She told me in the car on the way home when she was in second or third grade, "Hey ma, it's funny. When I go to school my friends say, 'Hey Emunah,what's going on ?' But my friends around the house say, "Hey whussup Mooni," and I can understand them both!" With that she busted out laughing like it was the funniest thing she had ever heard, but she had no way of understanding the deeply profound nature of her very simple observation. She was learning that she could speak and understand anyone's language and this would be a powerful tool in the world that she and her brother lived in.

We talked about everything from what people said that made them laugh to a math problem that gave them trouble. We talked about their interactions with their teachers and also those of the other students with their teachers. We even talked about what other kids were wearing. I made sure that no topic seemed too small because I knew that some things that seem small to children are very important to their parents. It was the closest thing to sitting in a classroom with them.

CHAPTER 6

HEAR O ISRAEL   שְׁמַע יִשְׂרָאֵל

Iddo's Kindergarten year breezed by in much the same way that Mooni's did. The kindergarten and preschool were attended by many different kinds of kids and the only thing that mattered was if their parents could afford to pay or not. It was such a great place to be that other black parents, who had seen that I had a kid in grade school there, wanted to know how I had beat the system. They wanted to know what loophole had I found that I could possibly share with them.

They would approach me with this question like we were running some kind of covert secret military operation. I'd be walking to my car in the parking lot and a parent would pop out from between the cars, or they might follow me to the neighborhood gas station or grocery store to question me. It was done this way because I was not the black parent that other black parents wanted the white parents and faculty to see them talking to. I was black, but I wasn't like them either. I didn't have a college degree at that time. I was young, much younger than the other parents, I had just made 25. Although, I looked five years younger than that. I didn't drive a minivan or an SUV; I had a two-door sports coupe. I didn't wear Dockers and penny loafers with a natural hairdo. I was hood and they weren't, or at least they tried their best not to show it, but I was something else that they weren't: a Jew. They had trouble understanding. They, educated black people, would ask me questions like: Is their father Jewish? Are they adopted? Or my favorite, when did you convert? I felt sorry for them. These were people who were by society's standards successful. They were doctors, lawyers, and some even taught at colleges and universities, but they had no idea that there was such a thing as black Jews.

That always amazed me. After hearing there was no trick to it or any loopholes, they never spoke with me again and none of their children would ever make it to first grade there. It didn't matter how smart, wealthy, or equal they thought they were.

As the years passed, my relationship with the school would become more and more contentious. The tuition went up and the payments were becoming harder and harder to make. I'd have to go in and literally cry and beg for extensions. It was a small school and parents on the board and active in parent groups talked, and everyone knew my business. It became so humiliating to me that I stayed away from the school. I believe that may have been what they wanted.

Every time I walked in the door of the school, for parent functions or report card pickups or even school plays, I always had to talk to the school comptroller. She always tried very hard to hide her disdain for me and people like me, I'll give her that. Right before she'd put the squeeze on me for more money she would tell me how much they loved having my children in the school and how much a part of the family they were and how it would just break their hearts if they had to put them out until I could catch up my payments. It didn't matter if it took three days or three weeks, which it sometimes did; my kids would sit out every day of it, falling further and further behind the other children and no one said a word about it, and I believe this too may have been part of the plan.

When the children would go back after their extended "breaks," it was difficult for them to catch up. Mooni always did, It was difficult for her but she managed with little ill affect, but it was different for my son. It wasn't so easy for him. He hated the place. He didn't like the teachers there and he thought they didn't like him. He was always such a man and I believe that even at an early age he began to feel what so many black men in the corporate world feel: the pressure of succeeding where others like him had failed. From the moment he walked into first grade he felt as if many of the teachers didn't like him. His story was the exact opposite of Mooni's. She thought everybody loved her. He was quiet at school, but at home he was extremely opinionated.

He was a savant when it came to knowledge of sports of any kind. He could remember facts and stats and details about people and events that had occurred long before he was born. He watched sports documentaries and sports news every day, and he was always a hit at the barber shop. While his sports I.Q. was impressive, it wasn't the thing that would impress people the most; it was his grasp of politics that would. After Sports Center went off he would watch the evening news with my mother, and later, he began to watch it alone. He would ask questions about politics and the way they worked. He developed a thing about presidents when he was about seven. He wanted to know everything about them, all of them. I bought books, we watched movies and historical documentaries, and he was always engrossed in whatever he was reading or watching, and when it was over or he had finished, he always had a million questions.

He began to factor in other aspects of history and how the presidents related to them, like wars and slavery, and this would lead to something else that he just had to understand. Within a few years he would use this method to acquire a depth of understanding of the American political system that many adults don't have. He understood America from its prerevolutionary days right up through hanging chads in Florida, but at school he was quiet. He was "slow". I once had a teacher call me in for a conference and advise me that I should have him tested for ADD or some other learning disability. I found her suggestion funny. I thanked her for her concern and was on my way. I think it probably wouldn't have gone so smoothly had she not been one of my teachers when I was a student. I still had a level of respect for her that I didn't have for many of the other teachers.

There were teachers there that I did like and respect because they deserved it. They were mostly the foreign-born and they helped me learn a great deal about Jewish relations also. These were the teachers I was always happy to sit and talk with during parent teacher conferences because it seemed to me that they saw my children the way that I did. They would tell me how well-behaved they were and how Iddo was the nicest and most helpful kid in any of their classes and that whatever he was lacking academically he made up with hard work. They talked about how Mooni and Iddo, were much more mature than the rest of the children in their classes and how it seemed that they didn't have the sense of entitlement that turned many of the other children into spoiled brats. They were good kids and they were smart,

Iddo wasn't perfect, but he was special and I noticed it, as did they. The teachers he liked talked about what a minch, Yiddish for a good person, he was and about what a good heart he had. They would tell me about him intervening in playground disputes, always trying to keep the peace or acting as an advocate for the weaker party. He never talked out of turn or disrespected anyone, especially not a teacher because that's not what he had been taught. He had what black folks like to call, home training; they both did.

They understood that they represented me and their entire family and they refused to make us look bad. They were such good kids that other parents would ask me, "How do you get them to behave that way?" I was always honest about that. I didn't believe in time outs or taking away things they enjoyed; I whipped them and that was that. They quickly found that being good hurt a whole lot less than being bad. It was shocking to most, but it didn't bother me at all. I knew what I had to do as a parent and I did it. They always made me proud. It was as if everything that I saw was wrong with me was made right in them.

It felt good when older women, especially black ones, would come up to me and tell me how nice and clean my children looked, or how well behaved they were, or how smart they were. It was a compliment of the highest order. All of the mistakes I had made and all of the feelings of doubt and self-loathing I'd ever felt disappeared when I saw how good my children were.

On the way home from school one day, Mooni described to us how she had forgone eating her sandwich that day at lunch because none of her other friends had meat and she didn't want to sit alone. Now she was hungry and she took out her sandwich and started to eat as Iddo began to share about his day. He told me about, d'aavening , prayer ,that morning and then about a kid passing gas during quiet reading time. I heard what he was saying as I was watching the road and the beginning stages of rush hour traffic, but I really wasn't as focused as I should've been. I heard him talking, but I didn't actually start listening until I heard the words hit and face. I looked at him and yelled, "*Who* hit you?" His answer was cut off by his sister, who had dropped her sandwich and begun screaming, "Just tell me who did it! I bet they won't do it no mo!" I was still trying to ask who did it, why and how, but traffic was heavy.

I had to calm myself and then the children down so I could get some sort of clarity as to what had happened. I had a lot of questions, but the most important one was, when this other kid hit you, exactly how hard did you hit him back? I didn't play that and both of my kids knew that. I believed in defending myself and I was sure that they did too. Finally, Iddo started to speak as his sister and I listened. He very matter-of-factly explained to us, "I didn't hit him back at all." When he said that, I thought I would faint. What? I had a kid that was afraid to defend himself. That's the reaction the hood had taught me, and at that moment I forgot the pact that I made with myself long ago, that the hood wasn't going to raise my children. He quickly went on to tell us, "He is an orphan and he always gets in trouble and he has a whole lotta problems and nobody really likes him. Even the teacher wanted me to hit him back, but I wouldn't because the Torah says that you are supposed to be good to the orphans and widows and his life is already hard enough. If I would've beat him up it would've only made it worse." "Wow," was all I could say. The Torah really did say that, but I couldn't think of one single time in a situation like that I actually had the presence of mind to think about God or the Torah before I was about to beat somebody down. Orphan or not, you hit me and I was definitely going to hit you back. But not my son.

He sat there and he looked at me and I could tell by the look on his face that he had no reservations about what he had done. He understood it and it made sense to him and he was looking a bit confused about why it didn't make sense to me. We were Jews: wasn't this the way all Jews handled situations like this? Sadly, no we don't. He was learning, and at that moment he taught me too. No one had ever used the Torah defense on me, but it made sense and it made me wonder why *I* didn't think that way. As a parent and as a Jew, I had more growing to do.

When Mooni started fifth grade and Iddo the second, there was the welcome addition of more black children to the school. They were in the same grades as my children were and they also attended the same Temple that we did. I was happy that my children wouldn't be so much in the minority anymore. On the first day of school, my children got in the car and competed for the privilege to be able to give me the news first: "Everybody thought Shawn and Tony were our cousins just because they're black!"

This was most interesting to me. Just because the children attended the same temple and were both black, the other students deduced that they must be related. This made no sense to my kids or to Tony and Shawn. They didn't think that all of the children at school were cousins because they were all white. They didn't see the logic in the assumption, but I did. The lack of diversity in the lives, in the school and in the communities of most of these children had taught them that all black people who have a common belief and are the same color must be related. I found that idea in this day in age to be incredibly sad.

When I was a student in the same school, these assumptions would never have been made. Perhaps it was because of the way that parents raised their children back then. Perhaps there was an older school of thought that embraced, accepted and celebrated the diversity of the Jewish people more, or maybe it was because there was more acceptance of difference in the school in the 70's and 80's. The other two black children didn't stay very long. They were there two years and then moved away. My children remained, and for the first time they became acutely aware of the fact that they were the only black children there and they felt alone for the very first time.

After that, I began looking around at other Jewish day schools in the city. I don't even know if I ever really intended on transferring them. I think I just wanted them to see that I was doing something to try to make them feel better. I looked around for a while and I found that with my search came an unexpected outcome. The diversity and acceptance that I was searching for in a Jewish day school setting didn't actually exist anywhere. Not in any Jewish day school in the whole city. What was even more disturbing is that this seemed to be the national norm.

Some schools had students who were bi-racial, but not many of them. Even in the context of the relatively small number of enrollees in these schools, the number of non-whites enrolled was still disproportionately low. I found that I was probably better off leaving them where they were, but I was still bothered by my findings. I started talking to people, other black Jewish parents with school aged children, to find out if they would consider sending their children to Jewish day school. We were all Jews; shouldn't we all want that for our children? I got many answers. Nearly all of them had the same issue that all Jewish parents have, regardless of color, when asked why their children didn't attend Jewish day school: the cost. It is very expensive for a child to attend Jewish day school, and one would be hard pressed to find a JDS where the tuition was less than $10,000 a year. Some charged as much as $17,000.

It seemed that everywhere I turned, there were things that would challenge my earlier beliefs. It was almost as if I knew nothing. I wanted to believe that Jews were different from other religious groups, but we weren't. If anything, there were facets of Judaism that were far more shameful than practices of other religions. It seemed that at some point Judaism had gained the distinction of becoming the only religion with a "face" and this face determined who could be viewed as a Jew and who couldn't. Perhaps this is why the Most High said, "Sh'ma Yisrael, *hear* O Israel," and not "See O Israel." Sometimes what the eyes showed us led us away from truth and unity. There were black Christians and even black Muslims, but it was totally absurd to suppose that there would be black Jews. It all seemed like it was by design; even if the Jewish "face" didn't exist, the supposition that there were no Jews of color still did. How could the fact of black Jews be understood when it couldn't be seen? This blindness was most evident in the Jewish day schools I knew, the first place Jewish children should be exposed to and taught about the diversity of the Jewish people.

I began to think that Jewish day schools might not be the place for teaching about the diversity of the Jewish people, but for teaching about something else: Jewish *peoplehood*. But what would this "*peoplehood*" be, and how was it determined who would be included, and, most importantly, who wouldn't?

Every year, the school held Holocaust remembrance ceremonies and they were sad and solemn. The teachers and faculty members would tearfully invoke the names of relatives who had perished while lighting candles and reciting the words, "never forget." Some of the students had grandparents or other relatives who had died in the Holocaust, but they didn't seem bothered by it much. They still looked at the ceremonies as free time. I remember some of my schoolmates supposing that since we weren't in a classroom reading or writing, now was the time to sneak and play with the toy you brought to school or whisper a joke about the English teacher to your friend, but for some of us it was sad, especially for me.

No, I didn't have relatives who were in the death camps in Europe, but I did have those who lay in a watery grave at the bottom of the Atlantic Ocean, and some who had been lynched and tortured in the south. I knew my history and how many of my family members had died tragically at young ages and how so many in my neighborhood died. Death was not foreign to me as it was for my peers. I knew its sadness and how bad it could hurt and I felt sorry for those lost in the Holocaust and myself and everybody else who at that moment was in mourning. Most of the other students did not share in this larger feeling of grief. They didn't feel bad for me or my losses, or those of anyone else. It was only about the Jews that were killed in the Holocaust; no one else mattered. It was my hurt and then it was their hurt. Theirs had a day of national remembrance and it always superseded everyone else's. Their hurt was always deeper than everyone else's. They had suffered more damage than anyone in the world ever had. They used words like annihilation, extermination and genocide, very big words for little kids to understand. Yet they only used them when talking about the Holocaust, never about any other group who ever suffered any of those things.

At school we were reminded that if Jews didn't stay vigilant it could happen to *us* again. But I had no ties to Europe or the Holocaust, and it was difficult for people at my school to think of me as part of *those* Jewish people. Every year we were reminded how it could happen to *them*, again, and how *they* had to always keep watch. As a kid, I had no idea what kind of affect this would have on them or me, but as we became adults and I became a parent, its affects would become increasingly more apparent.

I was saddened to see that even now the school didn't teach anything about the horrible acts of genocide that had been inflicted upon many other peoples around the world. There was never any talk of the hardships suffered by other groups, only the Jews. It was always that way, but it wasn't as much of a problem for me as a student as it was for me as a parent. It looked to me as if the school had started using the Holocaust to unite or build a "peoplehood" around, and if you didn't have relatives that died there, then you couldn't possibly be afraid of it happening again. If you weren't afraid of it happening again, then how could you guard it from happening? This is how my children were viewed. They were never really part of those Jews; we were never really a part of those Jews; we were Jews, just not like everyone else. Not *real* Jews.

This would become painfully clear years later, when Mooni was in eighth grade and, in order to settle a dispute between herself and two other girls, the principal of the school warned the other girls in her class to remember what happened to the Jews when Switzerland didn't stand up against Hitler, She later explained that she simply meant that "neutrality is a fallacy" and the other girls shouldn't sit by and allow Mooni to swear at her classmates.

The children in the school were very close and there weren't very many of them. At any given time there were perhaps maybe a hundred children in the entire first through eighth grade. They learned together, they played together, they had sleepovers and everyone was invited to everyone's bar and baht mitzvah, regardless of whether the two children were close or not. The parents socialized outside of school. The school prided itself on its close-knit community. It was great for kids to be educated in an environment like that and that is why I wanted my children there. I wanted that kind of a warm environment, the same one I had had, but things had changed.

When I was there, there were all kinds of students, and we were allowed to play together, work together, and the girls were even allowed to lead prayers. In all of this there was a closeness, but there was always an underlying spirit of competition. It was boy against girl, math geek versus math geek, Torah nerd versus Torah nerd; it was always there. The only thing that it never was was a racial thing, because the student body was mixed. If you were a smart black kid you probably weren't the only one. There were black math and Torah geeks, and there were also a couple of Asian ones, even a few bi-racial ones, and everyone wanted to be better than everyone else. We were friends, but we weren't afraid of competition.

When Mooni was in fifth grade, I went in for a parent-teacher conference. I was always happy to do that because I loved hearing the wonderful reports of my children's progress. I walked in the classroom smiling and sat down with her Chumash (Bible) teacher. He was a rabbi, but not an old man. He looked to be in his mid- to late thirties, not much older than me, but shorter. He wore thin-rimmed glasses with thick lenses and a short sleeve white shirt with a crooked tie. He walked over to his desk and fumbled with his papers, nervously trying to find Mooni's. There was a discomfort in the room that I was familiar with, but didn't quite understand. He and I had spoken in passing, but had never formally met, so I couldn't understand why he would be so tense around me. It would soon all make sense.

He sat down at the small desk across from the one that I was sitting at and echoed the words of every other teacher that had spoken with me regarding Mooni that evening. He told me she was very smart and a hard worker, and she was always respectful and prepared. This was nothing new for me, but it still made me proud. He went on about her for another minute or so and then the other shoe dropped: he suggested I was giving Mooni too much help with her homework, or even doing it for her. Where was this coming from? It didn't take long for me to stop scratching my head before I pounced. I understood everything now, the nervousness, the avoidance of eye contact, and most of all, the point that, I am certain, took him all day to get up the nerve to make. I didn't answer right away; I just sat there thumbing through the stack of A's, B's, and smiley faces on the papers in front of me. I picked a few out and then I began to ask questions myself. I held up one paper and I asked, "Did she do this in class?" He said yes. I then held up another and asked, "Is this a test?" Again, a yes. I pointed to the A at the top and asked, "Is this an A?" He replied yes again. I asked him, "If her school work is just as good as her homework, why would you think I would have to do it for her?" He stammered along for a minute and began to try to explain that his intent was not to imply that I did her homework for her, only to say that if I did, it was not helping her. He could see that I thought he was as foolish as he knew he sounded and looked right then. I was happy leaving him that way. Later on that night and many times since then, I have thought of this exchange and realized over and over again that he simply could not believe his own eyes or judgment. There just had to be a better explanation for how a black kid could be this smart. Sadly enough, he wasn't or isn't the only person who thought that way. I would see it in other places over and over again.

CHAPTER 7

GET THEE OUT   לֶךְ־לְךָ

In 2006, my Uncle David started to get sick. He had never been in good health, but he never showed it. He was a double amputee and he had many health problems that came along with it. He was mostly bedridden and didn't attend temple services anymore because he didn't want to go to services under the influence of pain medication or other drugs. He had been in a wheelchair since he was nineteen years old and he was sixty-three now. When he first sustained his injuries, the doctors didn't expect him to make it through the year, and he didn't either. Until he found his greater purpose, he felt that he had been broken by his injury and he was better off dead. In struggling to discover what his new life would be, he lost the old David and found the one he was always meant to be.

Although he had always had health problems, in 2006 there were more visits to the hospital and longer stays each time. There were new infections and more medications. His health was declining and I could see it, but David having always been my teacher, meant to use his own death to teach me yet another lesson.

I didn't go to the hospital and visit him much. I couldn't take it. I knew what was happening and I believe that had I been a daily visitor I would've begged him to stay and fight harder and longer, and I know that he would have done that for me. He loved me so much that I would have held him here. I would have held him because I didn't know how to live without him. I didn't know how to live without his support for everything I did. I couldn't live without my teacher, the person who first gave me a glimpse of myself. I couldn't live without the best friend that always made my birthday special and was proud of anything I did. I couldn't live without all of the things that I knew one day I would have to, so I stayed away. I know that he knew this because he was feeling the same way. He hated to see me cry and my tears certainly would've held him captive. Staying away was the only way that I could be fair to him.

As he got sicker and sicker, I studied more and more. I read books on kabbalah and studied what the sages had to say about death. I needed something that would help me get through what was happening and help me understand what was going to happen. I needed this understanding; I needed my faith right now. My family was at the hospital on a regular basis and I don't know what any of them were saying or feeling or praying for, but I wasn't there and it did not go unnoticed. I couldn't explain why to my family. Perhaps I didn't have the words for it at that time, or perhaps I just didn't think they would understand. Either way, this would become another defining moment for me and my family. I had been preparing myself; David had been preparing me for this all my life. I was learning to cling to my faith and to God. I had seen him turn to his books and his faith and draw strength from them on many occasions. I had watched him whip out the Bible, lick the tips of his fingers and turn a couple of pages and quiet whole rooms of detractors. I had saw the many times his faith had been challenged by some who had no faith at all just because it was so different, and I saw him put them in their place. It was my turn to lean on what I had learned, what I knew to be not just my truth, but *our* truth. It wasn't easy. One Saturday afternoon, I got a phone call from one of my cousins. She told me that they had to put a feeding tube into my uncle because he couldn't eat on his own anymore. I was alarmed; it had never been quite this bad. I got in my car and drove to the hospital as quickly as I could. I cried all the way there. I begged God for mercy. If he was going to take David, let it be like a rabbi once wrote, "like taking a strand of hair from a glass of milk," or let him recover and come home and be well and stay well, dying peacefully in his sleep at ninety-nine. I got to the hospital and when I saw him, I knew this wouldn't be. He was awake when I got there and of course he tried to speak to me, and he could see that I had been crying. He was so frail and gray and tired, but he tried to perk up for me. I fought back tears because I knew what they would do to him. I just held his hand and it was like we were having a conversation. I knew what was happening and so did he. This was the part that scared me the most, but at the same time, it gave me comfort that he was not afraid. He was going and I had to be strong and do what he would've wanted done, no matter what. I wouldn't let him down. I couldn't; it was too important. I kissed him on his stubbly cheek and smiled and told him how much I loved him and left. Before I could get to the elevator, my face was already soaked with tears. I knew what had just happened. I felt it and so did he. He had prepared me as much as he could, but there's never really any preparation one can make for something like this. As soon as I left the hospital, I went to my Temple. I was a wreck. I found my rabbi in his quarters and shared with him what exactly was happening. He was deeply affected by all of this too because he was an old friend of my uncle's. We prayed together and I got an anointing, and then we sat down and talked. For the first time the question of a funeral had arisen. I would never have broached the subject with my family because they surely would've thought it premature and pessimistic but it needed to be addressed. My uncle was a Jew. He lived as one and he would die as one. The rabbi gave me some pamphlets for a Jewish funeral home and we discussed the days to come and what needed to be done. I felt like I was preparing myself to do something for my uncle that he may not be able to do for himself, remind everyone of who he was. Soon thereafter, early one morning I got the phone call. My mother was crying as she told me the doctors said it wouldn't be long. I had heard those words two years earlier when my Uncle Larry died from prostate cancer while holding my hand on a rainy Saturday afternoon in April. I didn't even get that kind of warning just a year earlier when my Aunt Joyce suddenly passed on, nine months to the day after her brother Larry, this time was different. It was my uncle David–my father David. My children and I drove to the hospital not saying anything. I'm not even sure if they really understood what was about to happen, but they could see that something was wrong and they wanted to be there for me. When we walked into the hospital, I sat them down in the family room and went directly to where my uncle was. When I peeked around the corner, I saw that he was already gone. I knew that look. The room was dark, the machines were going, but he wasn't there. He wasn't legally pronounced for another three or so hours but you know that thing that you feel when someone walks in the room and your back is turned to the door, yet you can still feel their presence? That wasn't there and neither was anyone else. I had a brief moment before everyone got there, just the two of us, and I believe this is when he gave me peace and a bit of his strength. By this time my family had arrived in droves. Everyone was there, even the children. My uncle's oldest daughter Elisha, who has always been more like my sister, had power of attorney, so she had been given charge of making all of the decisions. She loved her father; she took care of him in a way that was so selfless that one would've thought he was her own child. She would now have to make the hardest choice she would ever make. The doctors told us there was nothing else they could do for David and they could give him a drug that would let him slip away peacefully, but first she would have to sign. How does one make a decision like this? What do you do? "Wait a minute", I thought. If he's leaving, he's going the right way. I called for his Tallit and his Kippah, found a siddur, and begin reciting the sh'ma. I made a call and the rabbi was on his way. I felt as if David had taken us all into another realm with him, and I wondered if everyone was feeling the same, or if it was just me. I just knew that in the midst of all of the crying and grief there were things that had to be done. While waiting on the rabbi, I overheard conversations between our family members about things that might still save him even though the doctors didn't think it was possible. They weren't ready to let David go even though he had let go. I was ready for him to be free from everything that had held him back for so long, including his body. I was sad, but I also understood the liberation he would finally get that he so badly deserved. I didn't want to sound negative, so I didn't share my thoughts. Like everyone else there, I was much more afraid of what my world would be like without him in it than I actually was of the world he was going to. In the grip of grief and fear, we sometimes are unable to differentiate between the two. I could. I didn't want him to stay because I knew that he wanted and deserved to go. He had stayed here a very long time for me and for others, and I knew this was what he wanted for himself. I walked around quietly and watched and listened until the rabbi arrived. He called us all into the room with my uncle and we crowded in around the bed where he lay with his tallit and Kippah on. The rabbi took a vial of oil out of his pocket and rubbed it across his forehead and his temples and then he opened up the rabbi's handbook and began to pray. The room was silent except for occasional sobs and the droning of the Vadui (confession) being chanted in Hebrew. The rabbi and I were the only two in the room who knew what he was saying, but everybody could feel it. They knew we were saying goodbye. As the rabbi began to chant the sh'ma, I started to wail: not cry, but wail. As prepared as I had thought I was, I could never be. My uncle was going and I didn't know if he was waiting on those words to give him the courage. After I pulled myself together, Elisha looked at me, I nodded and put my hand on her shoulder, and with that she signed the paper and the machines that were breathing for my uncle were shut off. I knew what I had to do then. The rabbi had told my cousin that I knew what to do next. She trusted me because she knew that I was David's apprentice and I would do things exactly the way that he would've wanted them done. I walked out of the hospital. I wasn't there when they pronounced him. I didn't need to see that part. As soon as I heard he had transitioned, I dialed the Jewish funeral home. It was a little after one o'clock on a hot Thursday afternoon in August and the Shabbat was the next day, so things had to be done quickly. This was the first Jewish funeral that I had ever been a part of putting together and it had to be done perfectly; it was for David. After I hung up with the funeral home, I went back into the hospital and into the room where my family still hovered over my uncle's body. I looked at my cousin and told her simply, "they're on the way". I then told everyone that they should spend as much time with David right now as they could because this would be the last time we'd see him on this side. Talk about an awkward moment. What do you mean, the last time? I was asked. Y'all gonna have a closed casket? The questions went on and I could see there would be no answers that anyone except for the other Jews in the room would like. First of all, there was a problem that it was me, the detached pessimist, doing all of the talking. I wasn't doing the talking because I wanted to, but because I had been asked to. I had an understanding of what my uncle would've wanted that no one else did, and my cousin who knew that I loved him and would respect his wishes enlisted my help for those very reasons. It was the beginning of an extremely tumultuous time for me. The undertakers came to the hospital and I think a couple of people even stuck around just out of sheer curiosity. I had never seen undertakers come to the hospital either. Before we left the hospital, we had picked out the casket, given them all the items that he needed to be buried with, and set the time and date for the services. Since the Sabbath was the next day, the funeral had to be pushed to Sunday, which was not as quick as most Jewish funerals, but way too quick for your average black Christian. When I say all hell broke loose, I mean *all* hell broke loose! I know that had everything been done the way people expected, according to Christian tradition, there wouldn't have been a cross word said. We had two and a half days to get everything done. The memorial service was on Sunday, but he had to be buried Monday morning. There had to be a program put together and arrangements for people to come from out of town, phone calls to be made, a repast to plan, and I was still sad. But I couldn't grieve; I had a job to do. I went into the bubble. The bubble meant all of the threatening phone calls and bad words that everyone except for my mother and my uncle's daughters Elisha and Denise, seemed to have for me did not get through. Once again, I had become persona non grata to my family. They hated me and I don't even think they knew why, but it all sounded familiar. Once again, someone in our family was doing something that wasn't popular and didn't make sense to most. Someone was breaking with tradition and no one asked why or even really cared because they just didn't understand. It took multiple conversations for me to explain to the black-owned cemetery where our family has traditionally been buried just why I needed a vault with no bottom and three shovels. First they had to find out if it was even legally possible to have a bottomless vault then they didn't know if they had three shovels! They wanted to know why I had all of these strange requests and when I told them David was a Jew and the burial needed to be Kosher, the lady asking the questions was absolutely fascinated and was happy to tell me they would do whatever needed to be done because he would be the first Jew ever buried there. David would've gotten a kick out of that. If the cemetery had questions, my family must have too, but they were just too angry or hurting too badly to ask. I would've been happy to tell them that David wouldn't have wanted an open coffin because he didn't like for people to stare at him. It wasn't that we were being cheap or cutting corners by burying him in a plain pine box instead of a more ornate steel casket; it's just that steel is used to make weapons that take life and in addition it doesn't disintegrate the way that wood does and the coffin should aid in the body returning to dust as quickly as possible. The casket we chose was assembled with grooves and pegs and had no metal at all so that everything could return from which it came. It wasn't that I was happy to see him go, but Jews don't embalm, so he had to be buried quickly. A Jewish body is sat with and prayed over from the time one dies to the time it is interred, never left unattended. I heard someone say that David's body not being able to come into the sanctuary at our Temple was disrespectful. They had no idea how much respect David had been shown this way and no one asked. No Jew alive or dead would want to desecrate the sanctuary of their Temple and that is precisely what would've been done had his body been bought in and David wouldn't have wanted that. The drama got worse and worse by the day. There was the anger at me for taking over and doing only what I wanted to do. There was a fiasco over an obituary that I only contributed to. There were threats of bodily harm because a flight had been booked with a layover, and it was supposed I had done that on purpose to inconvenience someone. It got so bad that my cousin, in an effort to keep the peace, paid a great deal of extra money to have the funeral home drive my uncle's body to our Temple just to sit outside with the engine running and the air conditioner on for the duration of the memorial service. Yet, I was in the bubble and I was ok. I knew what everyone else was feeling, but it was obvious that they had no clue nor did they give a rats butt about how I was feeling. I was alone, but not really, I knew David was still with me. I stayed out of their way. People were confused when they came into the building after passing a hearse on the street to find no body and no casket. How dare they, some thought. They wouldn't even let him come in the building! Some gasped. The rabbi eloquently explained the concept of the Jewish funeral to the group and I prayed that this would help, but it didn't. The funeral service was riddled with sniping and unkind words. There were parts that were even downright disrespectful and did a horrible disservice to my uncle's memory, but it was ok. I was still in the bubble. It was even rumored that someone there wanted to fight me in the Temple after the service. I thought it was all insane. After the funeral, I gathered up my children and I left. I didn't stay for the repast. I didn't go into the hall and fellowship with our guest and friends of my uncle's. I didn't eat chicken and cake with my family. I grabbed some take out and went home. I felt numb. I knew that I had to hold it together and the hardest part was yet to come. I stayed up all night. I drank and listened to music and tried to read a book. My cousins, the two that didn't hate me, called to check on me my poor mother called also, she was stuck in the middle taking the punches that were meant for me. I arrived at the Temple the next morning with my children in tow and the heat from the day wasn't the only heat that I was feeling. The words that the rabbi had said the night before and the seriousness of this occasion had done nothing to melt the ice around anyone's heart. I rode to the cemetery with two rabbis from our Temple and they knew me well enough to know that something was going on. They asked, but I was too ashamed to discuss it. I didn't even know how to, because I didn't understand it.

We got to the cemetery and the pallbearers lined up behind the hearse and pulled out the long light pine box and it was just as David wanted it; he was whole again. One couldn't tell if he had legs or not; they just knew he was a man and that's all. As we made our way to the grave, I noticed that there was staff from the cemetery that had come out to observe. Even in death, David was teaching. I was proud of him. The casket adorned with a single Star of David was laid on the ropes and the Rabbi began to speak. He threw dirt from Jerusalem on the casket and prayed and then he gave the go-ahead to lower casket. As the box slowly sank, there were sobs and moans, but they were short lived because when the casket was completely lowered the rabbi asked the cemetery staff to remove the ropes, rails and boards and bring us our three shovels. He then explained that in our tradition, we bury our own dead. We don't give that job to anyone else. He told us that this would be the last thing we would ever do for David and he was right. We buried my uncle that day as a family, but that would be the last thing that we'd do as a family for a very long time. I had already had a tense relationship with my family, but this would completely break it. I would never again feel like one of them. After that, the bubble burst. I left the cemetery alone, while the rest of my family went to brunch and from what I would later find out, everything came to a head. There was cursing and screaming and I had foolishly sent my children along. Yet, where I was, there was no noise at all. I had gone back to my Temple to tidy up after the memorial service and take down the photos from the previous night. In the midst of cleaning, I sat and just listened to the nothingness and I began to cry. I had just buried my uncle and he wasn't coming back. I had a whole life to live and it would have to be done without him and at that moment I felt no one loved me, or even liked me for that matter. I sat in silence and then I realized that it didn't matter who did or didn't like me as long as I did right by my uncle. I stopped crying and started to pray. I understood that just as my uncle had once had to take an unpopular stance in defense of his faith, so did I, and just as he never let the naysayers change him, neither would I.

CHAPTER 8

FOR THOU HAST STRIVEN WITH GOD AND MAN AND HAS PREVAILED כִּי־שָׂרִיתָ עִם־אֱלֹהִים וְעִם־אֲנָשִׁים וַתּוּכָל

The experience of my uncle dying had shown me a great deal about the things that were real and not real in my life. I had been accused of being a hypocrite, a cult member and everything but a child of God. At one time I would've been bothered, but now it made no difference. I became more vocal and observant, and I leaned even harder on my faith, my Temple and my God. However, I don't believe I was the only one feeling that way.

After years of caring for my uncle, my cousin Elisha began to come back to Temple. Not only did she come, she immersed herself in the Jewish way of life. I should've known she would because it would've been virtually impossible not to after spending so much time with David. She began learning to speak Hebrew and helping out around the Temple. She would tutor others who were learning just like her because she was always a little further ahead because of her rigorous study habits. She would pick people up for services on Shabbat who had challenges getting there. She was a minch and I saw that everyone there began to love her as much as I did.

She and her sister Denise were the eldest children in our family and they both took their responsibilities very seriously. They were the ones who would take me to school sometimes when my grandmother couldn't or braided my hair when it needed it, and they would even take us to the movies and to museums on Sunday afternoons. Just as I had found peace at Temple, so did she; we both felt closer to David there. It didn't matter what her reason for coming there was; I was just glad she was there.

Other than her and my mother, I don't think I communicated with anyone else in my family for nearly a year. I felt that I had been so ostracized and isolated because of my beliefs that I was left with one logical choice to finally heed the call. So a few months after my uncle died in the fall of 2006, I enrolled in rabbinic school. Maybe that was David's' plan all along.

I had thought about it for a few years, ever since I had watched the ordination ceremonies of two young black rabbis. I had known them for many years before they enrolled in the academy and I thought they were both capable, and I admired them. A few years after they entered the academy, I decided that I'd audit a class or two. I decided to do a Biblical Hebrew class and a Chumash class. I didn't stay long. The first class I went to was the Biblical Hebrew class. I sat at the far end of the classroom, out of the way. I took out a pen and paper, waiting anxiously for the teacher to begin his lesson. I was so excited. It had been years since I sat in a classroom and learned anything that had to do with Judaism. I missed it. I was participating in some of the Torah services now and I wanted to learn more so I could do even more.

As the teacher began to talk, it didn't take long for old lessons to start coming back. I started remembering things I hadn't thought about in years. I knew how to conjugate verbs and recognize the shoresh (root) of a word. I wasn't lost in this class. I knew as much as the men in the class. I found myself wanting to raise my hand many times, but couldn't ask questions because I was only auditing. I left after that class and didn't go back. I think at that time I believed intellectually I could do it, but socially probably not. It all came back to me watching them receive their smicha (ordination). I was proud of them and happy too, but at the same time I began to think, why not me? Why can't I do that? Why can't that be me? I understood that the academy didn't ordain women, but I still couldn't help but wonder.

Before I sat down in that classroom that day, I had never had any idea what rabbis were taught or how, but after leaving, I knew that whatever it was, I was capable of learning it. I was a single mother with many responsibilities and I took them seriously. I could provide for my children, change a flat tire, take out the trash, understand a football game and still comb hair and cook dinner. I didn't have just one role anymore; I could play whatever role was asked of me. Despite that women were not being ordained then, it didn't mean that it could never happen. I had never entertained the thought of being ordained seriously; it was unheard of, maybe even sacrilegious. I got to come to the Torah on a regular basis and stand up on the bimah, the pulpit, in the full view of God, shoulder to shoulder with men. Most other Israelite women were never afforded that privilege, but I was. Maybe that should've been enough for me, but it wasn't, and why should it be? I felt as if my development had been hindered because of my gender. Sure, I had been taught I could do and be anything I wanted, just as long as it wasn't this. I had never seen a black female rabbi and so it hadn't occurred to me that I might be the first one I knew. I knew I had to enroll. I had a daughter who had an affinity for Hebrew and Jewish culture and I believed that her strengths were important. I wanted her to believe that she mattered and it mattered. Her talents had value, even if she was a girl. I wanted all of the little girls in my congregation to know this. I had waited most of my life to learn this lesson. I didn't want that for them.

I would enroll under great opposition and criticism, mostly from men, and I was okay with that. I even expected it. It had been explained to me by those higher up in the academy that I was free to attend and I was welcome, and I would only be able to graduate, but not receive ordination like my brothers. They went on to tell me how there was a place for me as a teacher and mother in our community, but not as a rabbi. I knew of other women who had graduated from the academy and acted in the role that they were suiting me up for. I respected these mothers, sisters, and teachers immensely, however, that was what they wanted, not me.

I felt that I should be able to go as far as God's will would take me, not theirs. If there were things that I was meant to accomplish in this life, I had to do them, or at least try. I could not allow the fact that I was a woman to stop me. If I were going to fail, it would be because of my own shortcomings, not because someone else failed me. I went in knowing that I might never be ordained, but I wasn't deterred, I felt that it was what God wanted. If I were a boy who had been raised and educated the way I had, it would've been a logical and encouraged choice to enter the academy, but I wasn't a boy. Yet, I was still there.

My children were so proud of me. It was fascinating to them that we could do our homework together and that we could have discussions about what I was learning and what they were learning at the same time. Even though my work was far more advanced, we still could identify its similarities. I was glad that this was something else that could bring us closer together. They were always concerned about my grades on different assignments, just as I was with theirs. It was good for our relationship.

My son came home one day and informed me that his teacher had told him that women couldn't be rabbis, or at least they shouldn't be. Iddo was offended. He had seen my work and saw me do the same things that male rabbis did, so he couldn't understand this way of thinking. He felt that I was capable and deserving, so why would this teacher say that? He was livid. I had to calm him down by explaining to him that some Jews do things very differently.

There had been female rabbis ordained in the Reform and Conservative communities since 1935. Then there were some Jews who believed that women had no place in a leadership role in their community. People like his teacher were that kind of Jew. I had met and known and even once been taught by Orthodox women who were far more intelligent, capable, and qualified to be rabbis than any Orthodox man I had ever met, yet they wouldn't dare pursue a career in the rabbinate, no matter how talented they were or valuable they could be. It was sad. I had to explain to Iddo that I didn't have a place as a rabbi, at least not yet.

I became absorbed in the work at the academy. It felt like I was accomplishing something that I never knew I needed to until then. I needed to learn the things I was learning. I found personal meaning in all of my classes. If it were a grammar class, I felt good knowing that I was learning to interpret what I was reading and thereby deepening its meaning. In Chumash classes or Talmud classes, I could always find some way to apply what I was being taught to my own life. It was changing me. I not only was being taught right from wrong again, but I was being taught why wrong was wrong and right was right. It was no longer about me being guided by my own judgment, but by the way that we as

Jews had been taught to live since the days of our forefathers. Judaism, like life, had rules, and I was learning and being redefined by them.

I felt myself changing and oddly enough, at first it almost felt hypocritical. Even though I was making personal progress and growing spiritually and emotionally, I still was far from perfect. I still went out to parties and danced; I dated and made a mean pink panty (a mixed drink); I got my hair and my nails done faithfully; and I wore jeans as often as I could. I certainly didn't behave like the rabbis I knew. I still looked like your average everyday girl in my neighborhood. This was troubling for me. I tried to change my look and my preferences in certain things so that I would fit the mold, but after going sober for a month, wearing the world's most boring hairdos and wearing skirts on days that I didn't have to, Yom Kippur came and changed all of that.

I sat in the dark on the floor praying, and I can remember thinking how stupid I felt every year begging God's forgiveness for the same thing that I had begged forgiveness for the previous year. I wondered if He were even listening to me, and if I would bother listening to a repeat offender. I stopped praying. I thought about last year's transgressions and those of the current year and found that, while they were similar, they were not the same. I had actually gotten a little bit better; not much perhaps, but a little bit.

I had a few less people to apologize to and I had a little less guilt. I really was changing. I had learned and it had made a difference in me and in my life. I thought, "Huh, God has thought enough of me to help me be a better person", even me, with my blue jeans and high heels, highlighted hair and long fingernails. Whereas moments earlier I was praying prayers of repentance and supplication, I was now praying those of thanksgiving! For, he didn't see those things; he accepted who I was, both outside and inside. He forgave me every year. This was huge to me. Did my wearing pants somehow make me less than the woman who doesn't wear pants but defames her neighbor and teaches her children to do the same? Did my big red afro somehow make me any less deserving than the woman who bakes challah every week and observes the Shabbat, but is more obedient to her husband than she is to God? Did the clacking of my high heels somehow keep God from hearing all of my prayers? Probably not.

I had been around all kinds of Jews all my life and it was at that time that I realized that the majority of them didn't have a single mold, and

I shouldn't try to fit one. They were just Jews. They came from everywhere and from all walks of life and there would never be an outfit a hairstyle or anything else that people could see on me and say right off: she's a Jew.

I have worn a Star of David around my neck every day for many years, and there are people who still ask me if I am affiliated with a certain Chicago street gang whose symbol is also the Star of David, only theirs has nothing to do with religion. This is my reality. I realized that once again I was carving out my own niche. I had role models and guidelines and maybe even a few women who I hoped to pattern myself after, but none I wanted to be just like. These women were role models and special people to me because they didn't want me to be just like them either. They wanted me to be better. They wanted me to stand on their shoulders and see further. I understood that. I respected that and was honored by it.

It wasn't long before the novelty of my enrollment in the academy would wear off, although it never would completely die. I still received support from some and there were still some detractors, and sometimes people I didn't know inquired as to how my studies were coming along.

My children were both in the thick of elementary school in 2006. They had experienced life in the school and outside of the school, with other black children and without, and all of these experiences had begun to impact the way that they perceived themselves in their old surroundings. They were still comfortable in our neighborhood, but at school they noticed that they were not just like everybody else and sometimes they weren't treated like they were. My son had come to hate school, but at that time I wasn't sure if it was his school that he hated, or if it was just school period. Many children suffer from this condition; I know I did.

However, my son would drag himself into the car every single day, disgusted, and throw his bag on the seat and before I could shape my mouth to even ask how his day went, he would have already exclaimed," My day was horrible!" He never had good days, and after a while I would understand why.

One day, in the middle of the afternoon, I got a phone call that was definitely out of the ordinary. My daughter was calling me from her cell phone in the middle of the afternoon. She knew that that was not just a violation of school rules, but of mine too. She was never allowed to touch that phone during school hours. When I saw the number, I hurriedly answered the phone.

"Hello!" I said, and before I could say anything else, my daughter whispered, "You need to come and see about Iddo mommy. His teacher called him stupid and he's crying." Before I could say anything else, she had hung up. She would later explain she was in the girls' bathroom perched atop a toilet seat during class time, trying not to get caught using her phone. I was cool with that. Still, her news had greatly upset me. I rushed off from wherever I was at that moment with the singular desire of getting to my child. I knew how he must've felt if he was crying. He was a very sweet and sensitive boy and always went to lengths greater than most of us would to be nice and respectful and courteous. I know that no kid deserves to be spoken to this way, but my son really didn't. I was livid, and the closer I got to the school, the more angry I became. When I reached his classroom and poked my head in the door, I saw him, so little and sitting there with his head down on his desk. After a few seconds, he looked up and as soon as he saw my face, he started to cry. He immediately leaped from his seat and hugged me as tight as he could around my waist. I was crying too. I could feel it too.

He seemed shocked that I was there. He started to choke back the tears as he asked, "Do you know what happened today?"

"Yes, baby", I replied. He started to cry harder than ever. I just held him. He went on to explain that the teacher called him stupid in front of the entire class and he was embarrassed. That may have been all he could articulate, but I knew better. I knew that my son had been devalued and made to feel worthless. This is the way so many black boys are made to feel. I would die before I let this happen to my son.

We went down to the principal's office, and she took us in and sat us down. My son was still crying. I explained to her how much it bothered me to see my son like this and that I wanted to speak with his teacher. However, I couldn't. The teacher in question was conveniently gone for the day. That was probably a blessing, now that I think of it.

The principal said all of the right things and even appeared to really care, but that could've been because that is what the job entails. She was also curious about how I came to know about what was going on. I never told her my daughter had used her cell phone, but I think it was understood. What became clear to the school and to my son was that his sister would always have his back and that we worked as a team, and that she would risk getting in trouble for the sake of her brother. This was a turning point in my relationship with the school.

Nothing happened to the teacher. The rest of the school year would be tense, though, and it would grow more and more problematic over the years. Fortunately, the following year Iddo's dislike of the school changed. He came home every single day of fourth grade and told me how happy he was and how much he loved his homeroom teacher and even how much fun she made it to learn.

I began to see more and more every day what the school was, and they began to see more and more who I was turning into. Whereas once they had wanted me to believe that I was a part of this greater "school family," we weren't playing that game anymore. I had no desire to play and I let them know that. I didn't care about getting along or who spoke to me or who didn't; I just wanted them to teach and respect my children. The more incidents that occurred, the deeper I dug in. It was obvious to me that my children were not wanted there, but of course they always denied that. Who would risk a lawsuit and public outrage by making an admission like that? It didn't matter to me or my children what they wanted. The only thing that mattered to us was that they received the education and respect they deserved.

Perhaps there had always been problems there, and the one involving my son simply opened my eyes to what was really going on. I watched everything far more closely after that.

In 2008, there was a buzz around a black guy who lived in our neighborhood that was thinking of running for president. Not president of school board, but president of the United States. Many of us knew him and we had watched his career in Chicago politics. Many of us even voted for ex-Black Panther Bobby Rush instead of him for Congress. I knew Barack Obama, but I didn't start to take his candidacy seriously until it was time for me to do the first day of school tuition dance with my kids' school.

I was wondering what the comptroller at the school would suggest I do to get money that year. One year she suggested I stopped getting my nails done, and another that I should go out and seek sponsors. Next it was get credit card numbers from everyone in my family. Black people didn't do stuff like that. Perhaps this year she would suggest that I get a pole or a couple of pounds and a scale. I didn't know. I just hated being there.

She walked in and sat down and we started our normal overplay for the underlay. We pretended that we liked each other and maybe even had some measure of respect for another, but we didn't. I always loved the part where she would tell me–in her saddest and most sincere tones–how much they really valued my children's continued atten-dance, but that if I didn't come up with some astronomical amount of money in a matter of days, my kids, that they so loved would not be starting school on time.

This time was different though. She started to talk about politics, and everybody who knows me knows my politics. I am a dove, not a hawk. She went on to talk to me about how Ronald Reagan had been the best thing that ever happened to this country and how smart and decisive George Bush was and that it wasn't him that had made bad decisions; it was his handlers. She went on to tell me about how this guy Obama seemed like a nice guy and all, but presidential, nah, not really. She wasn't just telling me about what she thought of Barack Obama at that moment; she was talking about me and black people period. She had never once shared her right wing views with me, but she felt com-pelled to do so now. She wasn't giving me her opinion; she was attempt-ing to let me know how she really felt about black people and our "place" in this country. Whatever, she was attempting to do, she failed at it miserably. If anything, she caused me to look at his candidacy even closer. She felt threatened by the mere idea of a black man running for high office, and she wasn't the only one.

CHAPTER 9

GENERATIONS תּוֹלְדֹת

The candidacy and election of Barack Obama would do something to each of us on a spiritual level as Americans, even those who never claimed to be spiritual people at all. It would touch the spirits of each individual because we all are Americans. It would challenge our beliefs and our ability to be honest with ourselves about who we are and what our country really is.

Just the thought of a black president stirred up emotions in many that they were ashamed of, or perhaps didn't even know were there. How would you know how to feel about a black president if you never dreamed that one could exist? Many were forced to confront these feelings and they found it to be a life-altering experience. The same people who believed that they weren't like people who had a problem with other groups of people because of their race, turned out to be. They dealt with those feelings by becoming more hostile and uneasy in social situations where they might find themselves interacting with black people, or they let the feelings take them over and became like many others who would go on to become their very own political entity.

The anger that the country felt was so deep and so venomous that it seemed to have caused some sort of psychotic break. It was as if the whole country had become like this soap opera I used to watch, there was Vicky (the Republican Party), and whenever reality became too much for her to cope with, her bigger, badder, meaner alter-ego Nicky

Smith (the Tea Party) would come out to protect her from antagonist Dorian (Barack Obama). Dorian on more than a few occasions found herself locked in a cellar or an attic or at the bottom of a well somewhere for months, similar to the way Barack Obama became a president who many didn't consider an American. It was all very bizarre. I say Barack Obama and not the entire Democratic Party was representative of the Dorian character in this situation because he often stood alone. Never in my life had I ever seen a president vilified and treated as badly as this one was. It wasn't a hate heaped on all Democrats, and it was beyond politics. It was about the very soul and spirit of the country. There was no more out of bounds or going too far. There was no such thing. It became okay to be racist again, out loud, everywhere, all the time, and in the midst of all of the craziness, my children were watching, especially my son.

We live in Chicago, in the same neighborhood, just blocks from where the soon-to-be president lived and where Mayor Harold Washington once lived, and the atmosphere all around us was electric. No one seemed to mind how badly Senator Obama's motorcade would mess traffic up in the morning, or having fewer parking spaces in an extremely congested area. It didn't matter because we all felt like he was doing something for us. Even if you didn't know him or even like him, you did like what he represented. He represented a brand new day in this country with brand new possibilities. If nothing else, people were just curious to see how it would all work out. The closer Election Day neared, the more charged the atmosphere became. For some the excitement was like a kid having weeks and weeks of Christmas Eves, but for others it was akin to removing a loved one from life support on Halloween. Even as some were so happy, the world of many others was coming to an end.

The fear was that the world that they had known was not going to be like the one that it would become under the leadership of a black president. It was a future that was frightening for many, and they acted out of that fear. Fear can be a heck of a motivator for all sorts of foolishness.

The entertainment industry played a big part in the race. Rappers made songs about Barack Obama. Everyone from the more commercial to the hardcore rappers weighed in on Barack's candidacy. My personal favorite was "My President is Black." There was definitely a newfound sense of pride in the black community and I can see how that could be frightening for some. It reminded me of Mayor Washington's 1983 campaign, just larger, and this time I had a vote. Barack Obama was everywhere. He was on television, Facebook, YouTube, Twitter, you name it, and everyone knew who he was and what he was doing.

One evening after school I overheard my kids having a conversation about Barack Obama and the campaign. It was interesting. I didn't let them know I was listening because I wanted to see what and how much they knew. They were talking about a debate that they had at school and what arguments other kids and teachers made. It was obvious to me and to them that many of the children that they shared a classroom with weren't who they thought they were. Their political opinions and ideologies, partially shaped by their parents, were startling to my children in some cases.

They were surprised to find out that some of the children they had been friends with since they were in kindergarten would vote Republican if they could, even though they knew what Republicans stood for and conversely they were equally if not more surprised that some of the children there, fewer but some, would've voted Democratic knowing that the candidate was black. This was a great lesson for them to learn.

They saw what was happening at school and in the world around them and although they didn't always discuss it, they were always cognizant of it. They knew what ideas the adults around them had, but they had no idea that it had trickled down to the children there. The other children at school hadn't lived long enough to espouse Republican values or Democratic ones either, but they were old enough to look and see what Republicans and Democrats were doing and saying and to form their own ideas, but they didn't, and this was what was so shocking to my children.

Senator McCain and Governor Palin could say and do whatever they wanted; at the end of the day it didn't matter, because it was never about what they were running for, but what they were running against. This would change many of their relationships. The closer Election Day got, the more tense the environment at my kids' school became.

The night Barack Obama became the President of the United States was surreal. I believe there wasn't a black person in the country not holding their breath that night after the polls closed. I was waiting for the hanging chads, the ballot-rigging and the most terrifying, an assassination attempt, and I'm not the only one who felt that way. Black people saw what this meant. I suppose it must have been just like the day slaves were emancipated. Just as they knew freedom was their right, we knew that Barack Obama was just as much entitled to be president as any other American, black or white. We also saw the kind of anger that emancipation must have evoked in slave owners. They were not able to let go of the owner-servant mentality. They weren't willing or maybe not even capable of seeing a black person as an equal and definitely not as a superior.

Grant Park was full of people that election night basking in the glory of the moment. The last time I had stood out here was when the Bulls won the championship back in '98, and I tell you, it didn't feel anything like this. This almost felt like that night in 1983 when Harold Washington won. This night was still different. This night not only gave birth to a new presidency, but to brand new possibilities. There were new possibilities for all of us, not just black people. Sure, we finally got a chance to dream the impossible dream and I got to imagine that one day, that could be my son and his family upon that stage. I got to imagine that just possibly since the fight was over, so too would be all of the anger and hatred, but like I said, I was just imagining. This was a possibility for America to right her wrongs and attempt to make amends and begin healing, but that didn't happen either. Things would and have become progressively worse.

In the days following the election, we would see the president's motorcade going back and forth through the neighborhood and people would stop wherever they were and whatever they were doing just to watch our president go by. My kids were proud just like every other person who understood what the election of a black president meant. It wasn't just blacks that worked to get him elected or voted him into office, but his election would impact the black community and its psychology more than any other. We all found ourselves having to modify our behavior. There were discussions about the way blacks would be able to treat whites now that the president was black or if finally having a black president would make up for slavery or, in my kids' school, whether Iddo and Mooni were more proud than everyone else of Barack Obama because he was black.

I jokingly asked my kids if they wanted to wear their "My President is Black" t-shirts to school. "My President is Black" was a popular song at that time by rapper Young Jeezy. My kids knew the song word for word and so did I. My son was eager to do it, but my daughter looked at me and said, "I will not be wearing that. Why aggravate the situation?" Aggravate the situation? What situation? She went on to explain that sure there were other kids in their school whose parents had voted for Obama and supported him and supported his ideas and what his presidency could mean and she had to support him too for *that* reason, not because he was black. She felt if there were other kids and faculty there who weren't so happy with the outcome of the election; her joy could be antagonistic or could undermine her Jewishness. She had learned to restrain her emotions. She could be happy, but not too happy: just *as* happy but not *more* than the rest of the kids at school. She didn't want them to see that she was proud to be black because she feared that some would think she was more proud to be black than Jewish and she didn't want that called into question. She had to be proud of him on the basis of merit and not because it was an accomplishment for all black people and at this point he hadn't even been sworn in yet and all we had was the pride of a black man to ascend to the White House. We were bubbling over with pride, but not at school because black pride wasn't welcome there.

It was indeed an interesting time. We were getting a black president, my daughter was twelve and preparing to become a Baht Mitzvah and I was turning thirty years old. I wanted this birthday to mean something. Longevity is not something that my family was blessed with, so I felt that thirty was a real milestone. I looked at what my life had meant in the past and what it meant now, and while surveying every aspect of my life I realized that I had undergone and benefitted from my spiritual growth far more than any other aspect of my life.

Everything was tied into it. I couldn't succeed anywhere else in my life without my faith. I sold real estate and the market was just beginning to tank, and every time I'd turn on the television I would see a story about a real estate or banking executive committing suicide because they simply couldn't face being broke. I kept hearing the word recession, or worse, depression, but me, I just waited on Shabbat to come.

Shabbat was my own tropical island in time every week where I would take a vacation from the worries. This is when God gave me permission to not work, but to relax, go to Temple and pray. My Friday nights were reserved for having Shabbat dinner with friends and studying the week's Torah portion in preparation for the next morning's service. I lost myself in my routine, I needed to. I needed a time that allowed me to not worry about how the rent or the light bill or the tuition would get paid. God provided that for me before I even knew that I'd ever need it. The Shabbat became my lifeboat and I clung to it. I believe that in times like those, black people have extra reserves of resilience and faith. I can remember watching horrible news story after horrible news story when the economic bubble burst with my mother and her chuckling at that fact that it would take more than an economic catastrophe for black folks to start killing themselves after going broke; after all, haven't we always been in the middle of an economic catastrophe? Struggle was nothing new to us and we always knew how to adapt. I knew that one way or another I'd be okay.

My faith had kept me going for so long that I would celebrate my thirtieth birthday by going through the Mikvah, the ritual bath meant to symbolize not a physical cleansing but a spiritual one. I knew and understood what God had done and meant to me, so I wanted to affirm my faith. Judaism had been chosen for me by my mother, but I felt it was time to choose it for myself.

The mikvah pool was filled with rain water, which was caught in receptacles that sat atop the roof of the building. This in itself was amazing to me. It was hard to imagine that that much water could've been created by tiny raindrops, but it was, and it was right there. Prior to my getting into the Mikvah, I had time to reflect and think about if it was really what I wanted to do, if I really wanted to make the commitment or re-commit to this way of life at all. Along with the other people who were going through the Mikvah that day, all of whom were newer to the faith, I sat down before a Beth Din, a Jewish court comprised of judges who preside over the judgment of many different matters including, but not limited to, who will and will not be allowed to go through the Mikvah. It just so happened that one of the judges who sat for my Beth Din was the same rabbi who acted as the Mohel that circumcised my son. It was great.

After we finished the discussion with the Beth Din and were approved, we were individually led into separate dressing rooms where we disrobed, removed all of our fingernail and toenail polish, earrings and necklaces–basically, anything that God didn't give us. I am so happy that this time happened to be in between trips to the hairdresser. So, I didn't mind when I was told that I'd have to take down my platted hair and thoroughly shampoo it. I was instructed that I had to shower thoroughly before going into the Mikvah. I thought that was so profound. As squeaky clean as I was when I got out of the shower, I still felt as if there was some stuff that needed to be washed away by the Mikvah.

Prior to my going into the water but after stepping out of the shower, I saw myself in the mirror naked as a jaybird, but I wasn't seeing my nakedness; I was seeing all of the things that I would wash away in a few minutes. I was washing away any doubt I ever had or any of the times I took for granted all that I've been given. I was washing away all of the things that stood in the way of my drawing closer to my God. My mother wasn't even there; it was just me. I put my toe into the water. It was just about room temperature, but the best way I can describe it is like the weather on a sunny day in May, when it's what I call *nothing* weather: not too hot or not too cold, not too humid or dry, and you can barely feel the air on your skin. You know that it's there, but your body is at perfect peace with it. This is what the water was like. I could only feel its wetness, but not its temperature.

I stepped into the water and the rabbis on the other side of the wall began speaking to me. They couldn't see me and I couldn't see them, but we could certainly hear each other. They explained to me that I would go under three times. I was alone, so I would be going under of my own free will. Prior to going under, I was to recite the first blessing that was written on the paper affixed to the wall directly in front of me. After they finished talking, there was silence and I began to recite the prayer. At first, I was a bit taken aback by the way my voice bounced of the stone walls and against the water and seemed to sit in the air. When starting one word I could still hear the other lingering in the atmosphere. It was silenced when I went under into sapphire calm of the water where I sank until my knees touched the bottom and every bit of me from the soles of my feet to the crown of my head and every strand of hair was completely submerged. I sat for what seemed an eternity, yet was only three seconds. I floated up and hungrily gasped for breath nearly in a fury. I knew I had another prayer to say and felt a kind of urgency. I caught my breath and wiped my hair from my eyes and began to recite the second blessing and again, I went under. This time when I came up, the silence was broken by one of the rabbis telling me that this is where I could do my own personal prayer and before I could think about it, my lips were already singing, "May the words of my mouth and the meditation of my heart be acceptable unto you, o Lord." As short and simple as it was, there was nothing simple about its meaning. Most of us want the things that are inside of our hearts, that we can't or don't share with anyone to be the things that God hears. Our innermost thoughts and prayers and that's what I wanted.

I was making an offering that day: myself. It was a beautiful experience and I felt more connected with God and the ancestors when I was submerged in that water than I ever have. I had wanted to feel all the things I had read about, but I felt much more. I see now why the Mikvah is called "living waters." It symbolized a rebirth, an emergence from the water of the womb, and I felt it. I felt the newness and all of the possibilities that came with it. For the first time I felt like I was my own Jew, independent from my mother.

At one point it was vital to the survival of the Jewish people for the child to be whatever the mother was. In a place where Jewish women encountered so many non-Jewish men, the practice of matrilineal descent had to become the rule. This was because, as in Deuteronomy 7:3, the Children of Israel were led into Canaan and they would encounter other peoples. Although they were forbidden to intermarry, in some instances it did happen. Therefore, It wouldn't be about who the father was because sometimes paternity could be questioned. So the child became whatever the mother was. This is much the way it was for African-American women during slavery.

However, I believe that now in modernity it hurts us as a people. It not only acts as another tool used to divide us, but most of all acts as a tool to separate some of us from the very religion and the God that we, through our mothers were born to serve. The fact that our mothers were Jews makes us Jewish; somewhere along the line that became a cop-out to me and I realized it can tie some to the faith who don't want to be. It also keeps others out who have a genuine desire to be a part of the people of Israel.

I have learned from being both a daughter and a mother that I am absolutely not what my mother is; for goodness' sake, most women dread the day they become their mother, and I also want nothing more than for my daughter to be her own person. I would like for her to learn from the lessons of my life, not repeat them. When we are born, we are totally dependent upon our parents for everything, even spiritual guidance. However, somewhere in between diapers and Dartmouth, we change. We turn into our own people who make independent decisions. We turn into people who talk to our parents only when we are forced to and who don't go to Temple or even know where one is; we may even eat clam chowder and lobster tails or have a few tattoos, or hang up on our mother when she complains about our lifestyle. That is who the mother who gave us our religion becomes. So if this is what she becomes, then what becomes of the teachings she gave us? My mother introduced me to God and Judaism, but I had to find why it was important for me. I may have been born a Jew, but I was now an adult and just as I make adult decisions every day and am judged by them, why would I allow my mother to still be responsible for my decisions regarding my relationship with God or my spiritual well-being? Nothing else in my life worked that way, so why should the single most important thing? I was now standing before God on my own as we all should.

I felt the change and embraced it. I was open to the feeling. I wanted it to change me because I felt I could stand some improvement. After that, I was more eager to get involved with projects and people I wouldn't have otherwise been involved with. I tried new things like having dinner with people that I normally wouldn't and took part in community events that I may have once shied away from and whether they worked out or not I was still glad I had the experience. Later that month I would, for the first time, co-host an event called the "Freedom and Justice Seder," a few days before my daughter's Baht Mitzvah and a couple of weeks before Passover itself. Nearly two hundred people would pack the social hall at my Temple. There were Jews, Muslims and Christians all present in the spirit of community and *tikkun olam*, repairing the world, and it was beautiful. I have co-hosted every year since and the event continues to grow in popularity each year.

A couple of days later, it was time for what had been in the making for far more years than the age of my daughter. It was time for her Baht Mitzvah. It was bittersweet to me because the main people like my grandmother and my uncles David and Larry, who were an integral part of getting her there weren't there to share it with us. Yet, so much about the whole experience was typical for any parent, I imagine. Due to the fact my daughter is so smart, she felt as if she didn't need to study her portion much. However, I believed she did because in our community, the Bar or Baht Mitzvah kid has to read the entire Torah portion, not just excerpts. They act as the *ba'al koreh* (the reader) for everyone that day, and I wanted her to be sharp. The problem with that was she disagreed, and she thought her speech was tops too, even if it did sound like the teacher from the Peanuts cartoons. It was wretched. We had work to do and I wasn't going to let her rest until it was done, which was approximately a half hour before services started.

Many of her friends from school couldn't come because they were shomer Shabbat (strictly observant and didn't drive on Shabbat), but some did make it. Some of her teachers came too and I was proud to have them there that day. Our Temple was packed and we stepped it up because we were having guests. I was happy that finally the people from her school would get to see what kind of a Jew she was. I think that may have been the reason many of them came. There had been some curiosity. No one knew what black Jews were. They didn't know what we believed or didn't believe. They didn't know what we ate or how we prayed and they definitely didn't know that the majority of observant black Jews, especially every single one that attended our Temple, were more than likely far more devout and observant than most of the Jews in their school. We were not European Jews; therefore we had different *minhagim* (customs). Whereas theirs followed European customs, ours didn't. Ours were more reflective of the Jews of Africa. Many of their customs were based on rabbinic Laws; ours were based on mainly African customs, which were based on Torah Law. They didn't know of the struggles that so many black people had gone through in an effort to find their way back to our faith. Sometimes it caused rifts in families and severed other relationships and a complete unlearning of everything we had ever been taught. After suffering through those extremely turbulent times, the peace and solace that we found in Israel, was worth giving up the shellfish and Christmas trees. It was worthy of beginning a whole new life. Who we were had been hidden from us for generations by intentional miseducation, but once we discovered the secret, we honored it. I looked out on the crowd that day and have never been so proud, not just of my daughter, but of my people, who were there to support one of theirs.

The time came and there she was, wearing a custom-made pink and white satin dress and her custom-made matching tallit and head covering. The women in my family wore pink because it was her favor-

104

ite color and the men wore the white souvenir kippot I had purchased for the occasion. The men and women sat on opposite sides of sanctuary and most of the prayers were in Hebrew. We sang the Hebrew prayers in a tone that surprised those that weren't familiar with it. We had shofroth, drums and a piano, and we sang loud and proud, but that wasn't even the half of it. As Torah service neared, I could feel the butterflies begin to feel more like magpies flapping around in my stomach. I was nervous enough for the both of us. Today was more special for me than any other Shabbat had ever been. I acted as a gabbai every week, but today I would be assisting my daughter. My job as gabbai is to assist and correct the reader, but not today, because this was not just any reader. The biggest job I'd have that day was fighting back the tears. As we stood up there together, all I could think of was *l'dor v'dor*, from generation to generation. I had given the gift of Torah to my daughter as it had been given to me and I had taught it to her in accordance with the law, and it was her voice that God was hearing. I have never been so proud of her. As our collective voices echoed off of the walls of the sanctuary that morning, I couldn't help but cry. After she finished reading, she hoisted up the Torah, which looked to be as big as she was, and marched around the Temple to the congregation singing triumphantly, "We are marching to Zion, beautiful beautiful Zion! We're marching upward to Zion, that beautiful city of God!" One of the guests afterward would remark to me that they had never seen anything like it before and the joy they felt in the service was what Judaism was all about.

CHAPTER 10

ARISE AND SHINE, FOR
THY LIGHT HAS COME   קוּמִי אוֹרִי כִּי בָא

My daughter was now in eighth grade and Barack Obama was the president and I was still a student in the academy. My daughter was excited about the going to high school and she, much like I once did, started to feel that she was ready to go to school in a more diverse environment. She loved her friends at school, but she wanted to go to school with black kids too. She felt she had learned all she could in her Jewish day school. She could pray in Hebrew, she could speak and comprehend the language, and she had even competed in the prestigious Chidon Ha'Tanach competition. She had reached the pinnacle of Jewish learning and was ready for the new challenges that awaited her, but first she had to make it through the year and this year would prove to be the most challenging both emotionally and scholastically she would ever experience at the school.

The summer before eighth grade started, I began taking the children roller skating at the rink in our old neighborhood. There were no white kids there at all, who weren't being chaperoned by teachers on a school trip. It was a wonderful skating rink. It was state-of-the-art and brand new, but there was a stigma attached to it because it was in Englewood. It was supposed to be bad; there were supposed to be fights and shooting and sometimes, sadly, there were, but most of the time it was just kids skating. The kids that went to the skating rink were mostly from the neighborhood and the skating rink provided an alternative to the streets. Sure, sometimes they would bring the outdoors indoors with them, but it was mostly about escaping all of the things that they couldn't if they were just hanging out on the block. There was always security and I think most of them felt safe there. People just seem to be so much less violent or angry when they have wheels strapped to their feet and James Brown is playing.

I felt this would be a good place for my kids to interact with other black kids. They didn't go outside and play with the kids in our neighborhood because there just weren't many around. They got to hang out with the kids from Temple occasionally, but one day we were riding in the car and after overhearing one of their conversations, I realized they needed more exposure to other black children.

To my horror, they were almost talking about black people like they really weren't a part of their own race. They were talking about black people like their liberally-raised white friends at school would. It was crazy. I began to ask them questions about things that were "hood," things that they may have heard about in rap music and on television, and these people who I had regarded as very intelligent had nearly totally missed the boat. They listened to the music on the radio and interpreted it literally, and rap cannot be taken literally. This would be the beginning of us discussing every song that they listened to, so they would know what it meant. They needed to know that it was the language of the streets and, whereas they were a little more fortunate than others, this is where they came from and at any time could find themselves back there, so they should know how to survive there too.

Initially, when we started going skating, it was a bit awkward for all of us. Roller skating in Chicago is like a religion to some black people. It is a culture all unto itself and none of us could skate. Skating in Chicago means you can dance as well on wheels as you can in shoes and none of us could do that.

So at first we watched, then we got our own skates and got just good enough to look like we could skate if we wanted to, and along the way we met people. The children met other kids, but Iddo wasn't as much of a people-person as my daughter. She began to love going there. She met kids who went to public school and lived in the undesirable areas of the city and she still found things that she had in common with them. She heard their stories and began to understand that she was different from them, but not as much as she had thought, and definitely not as much as the girls at her school. What they had believed about certain kinds of black people, she had too, but not anymore. She was finding herself just as I once had. She was starting to realize that she wasn't all one thing. She was a hybrid, and I was glad she was finally getting it. She started to dress differently and she changed her hair, but she still went to Temple, hung out with her friends from school and could translate Kanye West into Hebrew. I was proud of her.

When school started back, I saw a much more self-assured kid. She knew who she was, but that didn't mean that she was ready for the realization that everyone else at her school not only knew who she was also, but some even judged her because of it, and maybe even disliked her a bit because of it.

This thought was too much for her to handle. She had been under the impression that all of the children there were viewed the same and treated the same, but they absolutely were not and it all became obvious a couple of months before graduation day. That day, my daughter called home crying, and through the angry sobs she demanded, "I want a transfer!" What? A transfer? I had never heard this kind of talk from her, perhaps from Iddo, but not her. I was frightened. I asked her to calm down because she was far angrier than I'd ever heard her. This was uncharted territory for us. She had gone completely and totally Englewood, which meant she was talking about whipping and beating people and she even talked about their mamas; it all happened so fast!

Once she calmed down, she began to explain to me that there were two girls picking on her, two orthodox twins. I had heard her talk about these girls before, but I didn't know them too well because they didn't come to the school until sixth grade. I had met their mother once, and she was everything that the orthodox parents at that school had shown themselves to be up to that point, so I never tried to befriend her, nor she me. Still, our children were friends until the day it all changed. The end began the day one of their teachers made disparaging comments about Ethiopian Jews that offended my daughter. In the process of defending Ethiopian Jews and her very own identity, one of the twins told her she was overreacting, and she didn't understand why his comments would make her so angry. My daughter explained that the very name of her congregation had the words Ethiopian Hebrew in it. Next there was an altercation in the gym over a game of kickball gone horribly awry, and finally, one of the twins made fun of my daughter because she didn't get into the high school that she had her heart set on. This event would change her forever and pull the proverbial wool from her eyes.

There had been words exchanged over a weekend between the girls on facespace or gchat or mybook or whatever computer chatting site kids were using at that time. I read the exchanges and saw it was nothing to worry about, but I told Mooni to terminate all contact with those girls and any who wanted to play instigator in the situation. I didn't like and don't like for her to be involved in drama. That Monday, my daughter went to school and before lunch she was calling me in a rage. A teacher took the phone from her, and within minutes I was at the school. As I walked in, I could see the looks on the faces of the other children. Whatever had transpired, they all knew about and it was as if they were all searching my face for a reaction. The anger of a black woman was something they had only seen on television and they were so hoping to see it that day. They expected a gum popping, neck snapping, finger waving, cursing and yelling shenaynay-type tirade, but they weren't going to get it from me. I got my daughter and left. I wasn't interested in hearing what had happened; she needed to calm down first and it seemed that just being in the building was making matters worse.

When we got in the car, she started crying, and where it had appeared to everyone else she was just angry, she wasn't; she was hurt. She was still hurting and embarrassed from the rejection of not getting into the school she really wanted to go to. She had no idea how the kids at school found out and can you imagine the surprise when someone ridicules you for something you never even knew they had knowledge of. She told me at first she was just shocked, and when she asked the twin again about exactly what she had said, the girl happily smiled and said, "Sorry you didn't get into Washington." My daughter explained that right before she caught a case for assault, two teachers grabbed her. While she was being restrained, she may have said a curse word or two; she said she couldn't remember. This was a big deal to me, because whereas other parents may allow their children to curse, black people don't. We call them cuss words and kids never use them when in earshot of any adult.

As Mooni told me the story, I understood that this was new for her and her feelings were hurt by people who she once believed had been her friends. She had no idea how to survive there under those circumstances at that point, but we were still just a little more than a month away from graduation. She had to hang in there.

She went to school the next day and I got a text from my son telling me that Mooni was crying and I should call her. I did and she didn't answer. She later texted me and told me she would see me when school was over. When I picked them up, she got in the car and before the door closed she was crying. She told me that she and the twins had been put into two separate rooms and that all of the other girls were taken into a meeting with the principal and teachers and when everyone came out her friends weren't talking to her and one of them was crying and no one sat with her at lunch; instead everyone sat with the twins. For the first time, she felt alienated in her school.

Later on that evening, after talking to one of her friends on the phone, she shared with me what had been said in the meeting that she or the other girls weren't invited to. She told me that a teacher had compared her to the Nazis and the twins to the Jews and that's why no one would speak to her. I was floored! What in the hell were they thinking? I couldn't believe that Jews would compare other Jews to Hitler or Nazis. This was never okay, and it would never have happened to any other kid in the entire school; the fact that my children didn't have the "Jewish" face meant they were never seen as being real Jews.

I went to the school the next day and demanded a meeting with the principal. Her office was nice. It had lots of windows that looked out onto the playground. She could look out and watch the children playing and they could look right back at her. This feature was the only thing that kept her safe that day. She invited me to sit down at the little round table in her office where she did conferences. She never sat behind her desk when she talked to parents, a psychological tactic used to make parents feel that she was one of them and could empathize with whatever issue had bought them to her office that day. It was like sitting around and having coffee with a friend, only we weren't friends, and I hate coffee.

When she sat down, I began telling her what my daughter had told me, and lo and behold, before I could even finish what I was saying, she interrupted me with a correction. "I said that!" She exclaimed. She, not a teacher, had been the one who made the comparison, and not only did she tell me she said it that once, she reiterated it three more times during the course of our conference. She explained to me that Mooni was swearing and cursing and threatening the twins with bodily harm, and they were frightened. She said she became angry and that that kind of behavior wouldn't be tolerated. She told the other girls that neutrality is a fallacy and that they would have to choose sides; they couldn't allow Mooni to talk to their friends the way that she had. She told them when Mooni behaved that way, they should stand up and tell her she couldn't say those things or do those things because (this is my favorite part), "Remember what happened to the Jews when Switzerland didn't stand up for them?"

At that point I wondered seriously if she could hear herself. Did she hear what she was saying to me? And if so, why would she feel it was okay to say it? Even worse, why would she feel like it was okay to say it to a bunch of teenage girls? What if this had inspired a more malicious or violent reaction in the other children, something worse than them just shunning her? Her words had inspired actions, and she had never thought about their consequences. I told her what was happening to my daughter, and she apologized as I expected, but what could really be done at this point? She told me that she'd have another meeting with the girls and see if she could fix things, but there was no going back. My grandmother used to say, "Let sleeping dogs lie," and school was nearly over.

The principal expressed to me her concern regarding the comments of the teacher about Ethiopian Jews. She acknowledged the wrongdoing of the other girls involved, and she would even admit that Mooni may have been provoked, but only in her office, with the door closed, around that stupid table, never publicly. I knew this and she knew I did.

I was so glad that the school year was nearly over. It had taken its toll on all of us. My daughter had come to a new realization; many of her classmates didn't like her. She couldn't put her finger on exactly what the problem was, but for a change she didn't care. Maybe it began after she and her brother had opted out of the school's production of *Fiddler on the Roof* because Mooni didn't get the lead role, even though it was her turn. Maybe it was after she stood up to an Orthodox male teacher, or maybe it was the whole thing with her being the big bad angry black girl who victimized the orthodox girls. She didn't know, and she didn't care. She was done apologizing. She told me it was obvious that the principal didn't care for her and where once it might have hurt her feelings, now that she saw how they didn't care about hurting her feelings, it suddenly didn't seem to matter as much. The twins wouldn't attend the big eighth grade trip, nor would they go to their own graduation.

After that, Mooni worried about how her brother would fare without her, as did I. He had never been anywhere without one of us. I was terrified. After what I had seen, I had no idea what kind of environment he would be going into. The plan had been for me to leave him in the school for one more year and then to put him into a gifted program in one of the Chicago public schools. I felt that with Mooni being gone and him having friends at school, it would make the transition much easier. Have you ever heard the joke that talks about how your making "plans" makes God laugh? This was definitely one of those times.

CHAPTER 11

ARISE! FOR THE
RESPONSIBILITY IS YOURS   קוּם כִּי־עָלֶיךָ הַדָּבָר

August came and the time of gleeful cheer that I've only heard other moms rejoice over was upon us yet once again: the first day of school. I was robbed of the joy that other moms partook in every year because the first day of school meant the annual tuition dance. Throwing myself on the mercy of the comptroller, the school board, the principal, the principal's dog, cat and goldfish and whomever else they wanted me to grovel to each year to get my kids into school. This year I thought would be no different, but it was. It had to be. It would set the tone of the entire year. Once again I had to come up with my pound of flesh, but this year they had my daughter's diploma and she could not start high school without it. I never thought getting her diploma was going to be a problem, yet it was.

I was told before school started that I needed to make a payment. I robbed Peter and made one and was due to borrow it back from Paul to make another the next month, and this was our agreement. This would get my son in school on time with everyone else and all would be well with the world, or so I thought. That year was one of the most important first days ever because it was the first time Iddo and Mooni wouldn't be going to school together, but I don't remember it as vividly as others because all I can remember is the drama that ensued when Iddo arrived at school that morning.

I had a doctor's appointment that morning, so I couldn't go with him as I did every single first day he ever had. This day my mom would take him, and his sister would go with to pick up her diploma, as she was due to start school the following week. What was supposed to be an uneventful morning became the fifth ring of hell when my phone rang and I answered it, only to be told by my daughter that they were not going to give her the diploma. What? I called my mom, thinking that perhaps I had heard her wrong, but it was exactly what she said it was. After weeks of stressing out about where the money was going to come from and how I would do this or that, I was teetering on the edge. I called the school and neither the principal or comptroller would take my call; instead they had the new secretary tell me that if I gave them an additional one thousand dollars, they would give me the diploma!

They may as well have said a million. I snapped. At that moment I let them know that I knew exactly what they thought of me and my children and exactly what I thought of them. I then instructed them to take the diploma and fold it into a tiny little ball and stick it wherever it fit. I guess they took my advice because I still haven't seen the diploma.

I would find another way to prove my daughter graduated from eighth grade and she would start to school on time. She was so nervous the night before her first day of public school she didn't sleep. I took her to school on the first day and it seemed as if she was the smallest kid there and I was once again afraid to leave her. I could hardly tell the difference between the students and the teachers. As she had in kindergarten, Mooni assured me that she would be okay and I could pick her up at 2:54. I spent the entire day hoping that she would call and tell me that she hated it and never wanted to go back. I had concocted an elaborate fantasy of how I would home school her and she would think it was so cool that her brother wouldn't want to go to high school either and I would never have to let them go out into the world, but that call never came and the dream was dead. I had to adjust to being the parent of a full-fledged teenager. FYI…I arrived that day to pick her up at 1:30; old habits die hard.

She loved school. The same week that school started, Rosh Hashanah, the Jewish New Year, came. Rosh Hashanah translated from the Hebrew means "head of the year," and it was one of only two high holy days. Iddo had these days off.

The day before Rosh Hashanah, I instructed Mooni that she should inform her teachers that she would not be in school the following day. She asked me why. This was the first time we would ever have a conversation like this. In all of the years in Jewish day school, she never was unaware of when holidays were coming or what was expected of her when they came. This particular day it seemed that high school had given her amnesia, or she may have been in the beginning stages of what all teenagers experience. They want to be who they want to be whether they are born to a Jewish mother or not. She expressed to me how she had only been in school for a few days and she didn't want to miss a day so soon. I translated this into adult as, "I just got to high school and I'm having fun and I don't want to miss a day to go to Temple where it's boring." After hearing my disappointment, she decided she would go to service with Iddo and me, but I didn't want her to go for me. It wasn't about me anymore. She had been Baht Mitvah'd and it was all about her, and her own personal relationship with God at that point. As badly as I wanted her to go, I wouldn't intervene. I told her that she couldn't choose to be a Jew tomorrow and not one today. I refused to write notes for her to be excused for the holidays that were convenient for her and sit out the ones that weren't. She was going to have to be responsible from that moment on.

Luckily, Yom Kippur, the other high holy day, fell on a Shabbat that year, which meant she didn't have to wrestle with whether or not she would go to Temple or school. Even though the calendar made the decision for her, I was still happy with the fact that she wrestled with her spirituality. Even though she sometimes seemed to be exactly like the other children, she was always awkward. It was never effortless. Sure she could fit in, but after a while she didn't want to. It caused her to compromise too much of what she believed in. She believed in forgiveness and being a good person and not engaging in la'shon harah (evil tongue); none of these qualities were much respected or accepted in public school.

Most of all she believed that even though she wasn't in Jewish Day School anymore or even going to Temple as regularly as she once did, she still knew what God asked of her: "to do justly, love mercy and to walk humbly."Each of us knows how that applies to our lives. She found another way to be true to who she was; instead of her attempting to fit in, she made others fit her. This of course is not a conversation that a parent could have with a child, but then again, I don't believe one needs to as long as they see it's there.

Meanwhile, Iddo was having his own growing pains. I had believed there would be some challenges in making the transition from being in school with his sister to being alone and not just alone, but the only black person in the school. Even the one part-time black teacher there had left this year. However, it became obvious fairly quickly that the school itself would have a harder time transitioning than my son did.

Since the time that black men were bought to these shores, they have been met with challenges that others would never be faced with. They have always been an object of fear and since they were perceived that way, the very thing that made them scary to the ruling class had to be neutralized. They were enslaved, and then their women were taken and made to become the mothers of the children of other men. They were beaten and sold and then they were further marginalized by having the rest of their manhood stripped away and given to the black woman. The black man has also been miseducated and imprisoned, and most sadly, because of bad schools and few job opportunities, he has been convinced that this is the condition that he is doomed to stay in. Leaving him in a state of learned helplessness.

Every day, I watched for changes and more stress. I worried about my son all the time, but every day he would come home seemingly unscathed. However, when he would tell me about his day, the stories began to become more and more disconcerting. He would tell me stories about his two friends whom he had known and been very close to since kindergarten. I had known them to always be very close because they had so much in common especially sports, or so I thought. Sports and their love of Chicago's teams had always bonded them together, but that came to a crashing halt the day my son came home and told me that he and his friend had a falling out because he believed that Dirk Nowitzky was a "way better" basketball player that Michael Jordan. Whoa! Those were fighting words to my son. If there were two things he knew in this world, it was politics and sports. Iddo said that his friend always thought that certain players who were definitely not as good as others, were better than what statistics or even their colleagues would have attested to. My son didn't like that his friend's selection of sports heroes wasn't based on facts, but on something else.

The something else would be pointed out one day shortly after this event by their other friend who was also white. He remarked that it seemed that Iddo's other friend only liked the people that he did because they weren't black and it seemed that he might be a racist. This was stunning to me. I couldn't believe kids were having conversations like this at school. My son told me that this exchange nearly ended in a fight, with him in the middle. He couldn't stand to see anyone fighting, let alone his two best friends. He intervened and played peacemaker as he always had and the problem was solved, but not before all three boys would learn a lesson.

I understood the thinking of the boy who loved Dirk, Brett Favre, and Babe Ruth, because I knew his mother. I had had an experience with her that gave further corroboration to my theory regarding the attitude of the orthodox toward other Jews and other people in general. As long as my son had been friends with this particular kid, they had never had a play date or hung out or slept over each other's houses. I knew this kid. I had known him since we sang the pineapple song I made up the day I put a pineapple top on my head and danced around with my son's kindergarten class. I remembered who he had started out as, who they had all started out as before the practices and prejudices of their parents had changed them, and this was precisely what had happened to this poor kid. What do you do when you discover the things that your parents teach you or believe in are not true? His parents may have never had a black friend, but he did, and nothing that he had ever learned or heard about black people could he see reflected in my son, his friend. How confusing must that have been? How must it be to try to stay true to your parents and what they've taught you, but being old enough to begin learning what was true for them may not be true for you? The boy struggled with this for the rest of the year, and I fear he may for the rest of his life.

My son would see a side of his friends that most children rarely see in each other, because most don't have to. He saw that one of his friends was his friend, but only as much as he could be, and the other was his friend absolutely and not because he took Iddo's side, but because he was willing to speak up and say something that was right instead of popular. Iddo was okay with letting both be who they were. He was just happy that he knew where everyone stood at that point.

Soon after, the second boy would seem to me to begin to reject Judaism because this incident was underscored by events that would occur at school that would show the intolerance of some Jews and he wouldn't be a part of that.

This incident would mark the beginning of a very long and tense year. One day in October I got a phone call at nearly noon on a school day. When I saw the number of the school on my caller i.d., my pulse began to race. It was never good news when I saw that number; It may as well have been 911. I picked up and it was a teacher at the school. His voice was very calm. He greeted me the way he always did; he was a quite pleasant person. He went on to tell me not to get alarmed (which always means you're going to be alarmed by whatever's coming next) but my son had had a run-in with a teacher and had asked if he could call me. The teacher had made a comment that my son didn't like and the he just wanted to call me. He wasn't sure if the comment had been taken out of context, but he said he'd get to the bottom of it, no worries, not a big deal. I wasn't alarmed at that point. I asked that he put my son on the phone and as soon as Iddo said, "Hello mommy," I could tell he had been crying. I could hear it in his voice and when I asked him if he had been crying he started to cry. I told him to pull himself together and tell me what happened.

He went on to tell the story that would be the proverbial straw. After listening to the story, I wasn't alarmed; I was downright pissed off! He told me that a substitute teacher who had been a sub for quite a while—a rabbi—had told him in front of the entire class that he could not be the vice-president of the class because that was a "job for a white kid." I asked him several times and in several different ways if he was sure that this is what the rabbi said, to which Iddo adamantly replied, "Yes, mommy that is what he said!" I made him tell me the story over and over again just to be certain that it was what it was before I acted.

I told him to put the teacher that I had previously spoken with back on the telephone and he could tell by the tone of my voice that this matter lacked the triviality that he had interjected into it during our initial conversation. I simply told him I was on my way to get my child and I hung up. I was there within ten minutes and the teacher that called me, my son and the principal were all at the door waiting on me. As I walked in, all I could think about was confronting this person that had said these things to my son. I was livid, but I would never get to place my anger where it belonged because as soon as I asked to see the teacher, I was informed that he had been terminated. This was very interesting to me. The principal, having a full understanding of the nature of our relationship after the first day of school debacle of just the previous month, knew that this could be problematic. She even remarked that we didn't need an incident like this. She went on to assure me that this kind of behavior was neither welcome nor tolerated at her school and that's why the punishment was so swift. She professed that they weren't even sure if the teacher actually made the comment or not, but if my son could make an allegation like this one they would absolutely believe him over a teacher.

I left with Iddo and the first person I called was my rabbi. He instructed me to bring my son right over to see him. On the way to temple, my son and I discussed the entire day and not just the event itself. It was very informative. My son told me that the incident took place during his first period class, which was at about 9:30. I began to wonder why they made him wait until nearly noon to call me. He also told me they never talked to the teacher and him in the same room at the same time. I concluded that someone asked this person if he had made the statement that he was accused of making and he admitted that he had. This was quite disturbing to me because if my theory was correct, this would mean that this guy felt that such a statement was acceptable at the school. No apology was offered to my son. Could it really be that bad? Had what once been my school really turned into this?

Things soon got worse. The next month my son was diagnosed with stress related headaches and he would sometimes break out into hives. He had to take medicine every day for these conditions. I even began taking him to see a therapist. However, he made it very clear, as did the therapist, he didn't need counseling. He had a keen understanding about what was happening to him and he had a great support system with his family and congregation so he didn't need to talk to anyone else. He just needed for us to know what he was facing there. No matter how wild the stories of his day would be or how unbelievable they may have seemed, I never told him he was lying or he was crazy or that such things didn't happen. I always let him know that I believed in him as much as if it were happening to me. I had seen so much at that school I realized I couldn't put anything past them. He knew we were in it together. I began to ask him if he wanted me to pull him out of the school; he always said no. One day he asked me, "What will happen to other black kids that might come here if you pull me out?" He told me that pulling him out was what they wanted me to do and he hadn't done anything wrong, so he wasn't going anywhere.

After that incident it seemed as if every day my son would come home with even more outrageous and distressing tales. One day he told me one about a teacher, a former Israeli soldier, who called him anti-Semitic because Iddo had said it was wrong when Israelis antagonize and kill Palestinians and it was just as wrong when Palestinians antagonize and kill Israelis. He said both sides had to see the wrong that they both do in order to make peace. I believe his views may have been a little different from his words, but for the sake of diplomacy, that is what he said. He was saying that both countries are wrong for their actions and both should seek peace without violence. How was this wrong? It was wrong because he didn't condemn all Arabs and Muslims the way his teacher wanted him to. My Jewish son being called anti-Semitic called for another trip to the principal's office and that damned table.

Each time I went, the tension built a little bit more and I got a little bit angrier. Whereas I used to avoid the school like the plague, because I didn't want to be hawked for money that I didn't have, I wouldn't anymore. I knew that they wanted money. That was a given, but I wanted something too. I wanted to not have to come and sit in the principal's office on what had turned into a regular basis because it seemed that they had no idea how to treat my son. They sensed my anger and no one said anything to me about money at those times.

The day I had the meeting with the principal about the "anti-Semitic" comment, she did as she always did, feigned disappointment in the teacher and nodded with a very pensive and concerned look on her face. I knew that tactic though; I had used it a million times. I look as if I'm very concerned with what someone may be saying, but I am really trying to figure out what their hairpiece was made of or was that a wig or weave, or something else arbitrary like that. It appears that I am really listening, but I probably am not. The same way she was not. She heard what I was saying, but she definitely was not listening and I knew this. I was always told, "You can't bullshit a bullshitter." I knew that; I just don't think she did. No resolutions ever came from these meetings. Nothing ever changed, but it was okay. I realized if something was going to get done, I'd have to do it. At that time I informed her that I would be sitting in on this particular teacher's class a few days a week. I felt that it would give us a better idea of what was going on and how we could fix any situations before they became problems.

I started sitting in shortly before winter break and it was a truly eye opening experience. On the first day, I went into the main office to let them know I was there. I then proceeded to go up to the classroom. I gently tapped the door and walked in; it was a few moments after the bell had rung. When my son saw my face, he lit up, but just for a second. The entire class was looking and whispering and the teacher smiled and invited me to sit wherever I'd like. I didn't want to interrupt, so I eyed a seat in the corner and quickly got to it. As soon as I sat down, the phone in the classroom rang. The teacher went over to answer it and it was someone in the main office informing him that I was on my way up. This would've not been a big deal at all if the conversation had been in English. I think they were under the impression that I didn't understand Hebrew. I just smiled as I listened to the quick conversation. It was too late; I was already there. It's good they weren't committing a crime and the other teacher was the lookout.

As I settled in, the first thing that got my attention was the way the classroom was set up. There were maybe four or five clusters of three desks a piece spread out around the room. The groups weren't all male or female. They were mixed. The thing that really grabbed me was one kid sitting near the corner where I was. His back was turned to the teacher and he was playing with a toy of some sort for nearly twenty minutes before the teacher noticed. There were only eleven kids in the class, which was why it made it difficult for me to understand why it took the teacher so long to get this student engaged in the class. After sitting for awhile longer, I noticed that there was one group of kids that always raised their hands, were called on, and then answered the question. Then there were a couple who just yelled out, and then there were some that the teacher just yelled at. Finally, there was a couple that didn't really fit in anywhere and were ignored.

This day that I visited was a few days after dangerous wild fires had begun in Israel. I realized what a sensitive issue this was for the teacher as an Israeli, but the way that he taught his opinion as fact to the children that day was extremely disturbing to me. I had heard that this is what he did on a regular basis, but seeing it with my own two eyes was just too much for me. This man, a teacher, told the children that Arab youths had started the fires and then once other Arabs saw what those had done in northern Israel, other Arabs went about trying to start fires in other places around Israel. He told the children that this was a form of eco-terrorism. The classroom erupted with comments and questions. Some of the children made references to Muslims hating and wanting to kill the Jewish people. Some asked if it could happen here, but what I heard mostly was there fear. Instead of this teacher calming that fear and dispelling all of the ideas that the children had that weren't true, he fed into them and took the children right along with him.

He didn't once think about what kind of adults scared children grow to be. Once again, just as I had seen my daughter being compared to the Nazis, there were now the Arabs and Muslims to be afraid of, and if you weren't afraid of the Arabs and Muslims you were probably not a good Jew. Try telling a kid from a ghetto full of Arab owned gas stations and corner stores that he needs to be afraid of them. Try telling a kid who has experienced Iftar and breaking of the fast at Ramadan with Muslims that he needs to be afraid. This was the problem with my son. I saw it clear as day. The same fear that held them together was the one that kept him out. When he got in the car after school that day, I asked him what he thought about that lesson. He said, "You just can't teach kids stuff like that. I feel sorry for those kids."I went back a couple of more times before school ended for the break, and it was much the same each time. I was happy to get a break. I was happy for my son to get a break. He needed one, even if it was a short one.

The break was a too-brief respite; the rest of the year would be hell. My son went back to school late in January because of money and the situation got worse quickly. I knew what we were facing, but I didn't know if my son really grasped it until the night before he went back to school. He came into my bedroom shortly before bedtime and he said, "I know you're scared for me. Don't you think James Meredith's mother was scared for him too? Plus I got a cell phone; I'll be fine." I understood then that my son completely got it. He had watched black kids come and go for years and he wasn't going to be one of them. He was on a mission and all I could do was support him.

Between January and June I'd be in the principal's office at least four more times and once because I was told that the same Israeli teacher that I had problems with before was scaring some of the children and they thought he might become violent. The principal told me, "Well, he'll be going back to Israel after this school year." It didn't matter that the children were afraid of him, or that he even told me in front of the principal, sitting around her little "table of trust," that he couldn't teach my son. He said it always felt as if he were walking on eggshells when my son was around. This would explain why my son would always tell me about how he got ignored in that class. I found myself in her office again, this time I invited my rabbi to come along, after another teacher told my son in front of the entire class that slavery wasn't as bad for black people as the Holocaust was for Jews. The teacher reasoned that the Jews had been killed and that black people had been treated pretty well because they were property like a house or a car. You wouldn't want to wreck your car, would you? As Jews, we should've all learned that it is never okay to compare scars, but that's what this teacher was doing. My son was very upset. He asked all of the adults in the office that day, "How do you defend yourself against other Jews when you're a Jew yourself?"

My son was having headaches more and more frequently now and breaking out in hives. This kept him out of school quite a bit toward the end of the year. The environment was becoming increasingly hostile and what he was about to do wouldn't make it any better. He had come home every day in February complaining about how they weren't learning anything for black history month at school. He asked every day if they were going to do something special and was told no. This went on until his Social Studies teacher told him perhaps they'd do something in March. March is not Black History Month. This really bothered my son. One day in late April, Iddo came to me and said he wanted to do something that would really get their attention. He felt as if they didn't care about what he wanted, so he wanted to do something. He then told me that he did not want to take part in the Yom Ha'Shoah, the Holocaust commemoration day. He was fed up and he wasn't going to take part in any of the things they thought were important because they didn't respect any of the things that he thought were important. He wrote a letter and hand-delivered it to the principal, informing her of why he wouldn't be in school on that day. He wrote in his letter, "I really got upset when we started to prepare for Yom Ha'Shoah on the Friday before the actual holiday. We could celebrate a holiday that is only one day long for two days, but we couldn't celebrate one that's a whole month long for one day?" He also wrote about how he didn't want to just talk about black people in general, he wanted to talk about blacks and Jews and the way the two have worked closely together over the years, especially during the civil rights movement of the 1960's. In addition to talking about Goodman, Cheney and Schwerner, Jews who died for the cause of civil rights in Mississsppi and Rabbi Abraham Joshua Heschel who worked very closely with Dr. King, he also wanted to talk about the Lemba, Abayudaya and Ebo Jews on the continent of Africa and all of the Jews in South America with African roots. This would never be.

I wrote a letter also and sent it along with his to the principal and to the board at the school and a few other people. To this day, the principal has yet to call either of us in around her table to discuss it.

His letter would prompt other parents at the school to meet and come forth to share their stories of what had been going on there with their children. Some kids were being bullied, some were treated differently, and there was a lot of talk about who kept kosher and what temples they attended. It was almost like they were religiously "coming out," but that wasn't what the students were there for. Listening to them, I could see that somewhere along the line someone had made them feel bad or ashamed of the Jews that they were; it almost seemed as if the parents themselves were suffering the same fate as their children. They too had sat around the table and received the lip service from the principal who never did anything. Up until this point, I thought I was the only one. Some parents thought that it was the Orthodox and all of their children that were keeping the school open and perhaps this is why they looked the other way when their children were mistreated at school. Listening to a few of them talk, I could hear a trace of helplessness in their voices. I wasn't raised to fear Orthodox Jews as they had been. I didn't have to grow out of it because I hadn't grown up with it. They wanted to do something, and for the first time they felt that they could.

CHAPTER 12

AND HE CALLED   וַיִּקְרָא

In a Kabbalah class that I once took, I learned of something called the "Glass Blower Analogy." Kabbalah is the name given to the world of Jewish Mysticism outlined in the Zohar. Kabbalistic thoughts and ideas are extremely difficult for many to grasp and this is why it is not usually taught until one reaches the age of forty or have sufficiently studied and can understand Torah and Talmud. Kabbalah speaks purely to the spiritual and not the religious. It goes beyond that. Kabbalah causes one to ask questions of oneself that they never could have dreamed that answers exist to. It challenges the mind to believe in things that are totally unbelievable but are the most obvious and apparent things that could possibly ever be. What is more obvious than your very existence? It's the how, why and where we exist that I have found that most struggle with.

The Glass Blower Analogy simplified this for me, and while it did not make me a Kabbalah master, it moved me further along on the path to where I need to be. Kabbalah explains that the soul is divided into five levels. The duties and purpose of each can best be described by the Glass Blower Analogy and it goes as follows: The first level is the Nefesh (resting soul), the Ruach (wind), Neshamah (breath), the Chayah (living essence) and the Yechidah (unique essence).

The glass blower himself is God. At the most basic level is the Nefesh; this is where we actually are aware that the body is a vessel that contains the spiritual. This is where the glass blower's air rests and has form. Another level up is the Ruach. This is the level where we can feel the motion of the wind of God moving around us. This is the wind or the breath that comes from the straw of the glass blower and before it cools and settles while it is still in motion. Still another level higher is the Chayah. This is the part of us that comes from the very lungs of the glass blower himself. This is the part of us that is never separated from God. At this point we exist in his realm. The highest level is the Yechidah. This is the very idea of the glass blower to even create the vessel, or the idea of God to create man, and anything beyond that is unknowable. I didn't need to know. I knew enough.

The teaching of this analogy changed my life. Even though I hadn't and still haven't mastered Kabbalah, I can safely say that whatever I was supposed to learn, I did. Something about it spoke to me. I had always been taught that I had a connection with God and that he lives in each of us. However, when I really read and understood the Glass Blower Analogy, I could see and feel just how. For the first time I understood that the same way he lived inside of me, I also, *we* also, live inside of him, in his realm, in his thoughts and his "lungs," if we chose to believe it, and I did. It was almost as if I had never believed in anything before this was revealed to me.

It had always been about the God on the outside, the one that lives in the world, the God that has to do battle with other gods every day, the God that I had to defend my belief in all of my life, the God that had been put into a box by religion. For the first time it was about the God inside of me. It didn't matter what anybody had to say after that. It wasn't about my religion; it was about me and God. I realized it's never about any of our religions; it's about us and God, but sometimes we allow our places of worship, our spiritual leaders, and even our own vanity to impede the growth of that relationship. I believe that it is because so many of us have not experienced this awakening and don't feel the bond that our actions go unchecked. We do things and think things when we think no one is looking and truly believe things in our hearts that we would never share with others because we know how wrong they are because we haven't really given thought to the possibility that we live within God and he within us. We go to great lengths to hide unrighteous thoughts and deeds from other human beings but we don't give God the same respect. When I acknowledged these facts, it seemed that some of the things that we learn as children about God, faith and religion are nothing more than well-meant old wives tales meant to civilize us toward each other, but sadly it doesn't seem to do much between us and God.

I then began to confront all of the things about me that I thought were shameful and I tried and still work on trying to fix them. I struggle with it every day, but I am content that God sees my struggle and just like I watch my children struggle with who they are and am proud because they do so, I would like to think he sees the same in me.

There were many things that I had to let go of, but before I could, I had to recognize that they were problems in the first place. We all have things we need to get rid of and we work diligently to kick some habits. We don't mind committing to trying to break the innocent habits like smoking or over eating or buying shoes and clothes that we don't need and probably are never going to wear, but too many of us have grown to attached to our heirlooms of ignorance, prejudice and hate that have been born and bred into us and we would never commit to giving those up.

On any given Shabbat at my Temple we have visitors. Sometimes more than others, but there are always some new faces and if my Temple is not the most diverse in the city, it is one of them. There are blacks, whites, Hispanics, and Asians who all come with their own unique stories of their Judaism. The funny thing about that was when Ashkenazi Jews first began coming to visit, I didn't think twice about it. I figured they were Jews and they were coming to see how we do things like I had done when we went to visit their synagogues. However, the first time I saw one of the Anusim (Hispanic Jews) at my Temple, I thought they must be in the wrong place. Are they really Jews? Before I could finish the thought, I was embarrassed, and as I write it I am still a bit embarrassed by it, but I need to share it; it's important. I had bought into the stereotypical look of Judaism myself: the prominent nose, pale skin and curly black hair. I didn't realize it until then. I had to ask myself about all of the times that my authenticity as a Jew had been questioned and how I felt. I had to think about how they looked different from me and I looked different from the Ashkenazim, but I was still a Jew and so were they. Who was I to say who was a Jew or not? How dare I? I had become exactly what I disliked and criticized others for, and I was ashamed.

I was born into prejudice and I have struggled with it all of my life. Black people were given Jesus and I was black, but I didn't want him. I wanted God. I am not sure if they are considered to be both the same or how they are related, and the worse part about that is that most card-carrying, bible-thumping, church-going good Christians don't know either. I know that because I've been asking for years and have yet to get a satisfactory answer. I'm sure the answer exists, but that is not my main concern. What concerns me is how easy for those who know and understand so little about their faith to challenge and condemn me for mine. Somehow it has become *believers* and *non-believers*. Just because someone doesn't embrace the religion of the majority doesn't mean the non-believer has no faith or spirituality.

By saying one couldn't have spirituality or be a believer without being a part of a religious community or a church, those who were simply spiritual beings were shunned. No one believed you could have God inside of you without Jesus accompanying him. Like it or not, that's simply what we were taught. The three went hand in hand: the Father, the Son and the Holy Ghost, and to question that was deemed blasphemous. Some did openly, and many more did only in their hearts, not daring to speak the words. The non-believer became an outcast at a time when a recently emancipated black people who were still searching for an identity started building their communities around the church. This left the non-believers their own place: the juke joint. What to most was a den of iniquity was also a place where many could go and find acceptance, on their terms. They didn't try to be anything they weren't because no matter how much they tried, they knew how the society that they lived in viewed them. To the whites they were just niggers and to the church folks they were the undesirables who you wouldn't take home to meet your mother. One of my favorite scenes in any movie is a scene from *The Color Purple*, when Suge Avery and the band and all of the non-believers burst into her father's church singing, "God is trying to tell you something." She sings the song as if her heart is going to explode and in the middle of this very stirring song she stops and says to her father, the preacher, "See daddy, sinners have a song too." That scene always makes me cry. That says it all. No one had *called* them sinners, but they assumed that's who they were because that's what others *saw* them as. They began to ignore God's voice in them and give into other inclinations, but like in Suge's case, sometimes it bursts out anyway because it's always there.

What would this mean for our community? By teaching that God can only live in those that live in the church, everyone else was left out in the cold. Just because all black people were forced to be the same in the beginning doesn't mean we were meant to stay that way. We are not all meant to be Christians, Muslims, or even Jews! We can be whatever our souls lead us to and this search is what those labeled as non-believers or heathens have been deprived of. Just as we have choices in everything else, we have choices in our spiritual matters. Going to church or a mosque or the temple does not make you better than anyone; it is supposed to make you better at being who you are. It doesn't mean because you're getting better that others who don't attend your place of worship–or any place of worship, for that matter–are getting worse.

The things that cause division in the black community do the same thing in the Ashekenazi Jewish community. I have seen the Reform, Conservative, Traditional and every other kind of Jew castigated by the Orthodox Jew who claims that he is the only Jew. If a Jew does not have a black hat a long beard with side burns and a black suit, God doesn't recognize him? I and other Jews believe that the very stance that many Orthodox take on their Judaism and the Judaism of others is more un-Jewish or trafe than any ham sandwich a "cultural" Jew could ever eat. In my life I've seen enough of those kinds of Jews to know that the majority of them don't live in God's world. They live in their very own world with a God that they have created, and no other Jews can ever really serve that God because we don't know how. Their God lives within an eruv and he doesn't like outsiders and he only sees and cares about the Orthodox. This must be the case because I am certain that such pious people wouldn't want the God that all Jews are supposed to serve to see the way they treat everyone else who doesn't live in their world.

All that I have learned thus far has prepared me to live in a world all my own, interstitially, between the borders of all of the other worlds that intersect with mine every day. I am happy here, although sometimes it does get lonely. I used to second-guess myself and try to find ways to get out and back into a world with a people who I was just like, but that world didn't exist and every time I tried to fit into one that did, I was forced out. If I wasn't forced out by other young people who didn't think so much like me, then it was by guys like one I once went on a date with who thought I was trying to start a conversation about a gang war instead of the war in Iraq, or Jappys (Jewish American Princesses) who believed that being friends with me would somehow help them understand the black struggle or prove to themselves they were more liberal than their parents, only to demonstrate to me that the apple doesn't fall far from the tree. It could've been any of these, but the experience didn't leave me bitter; it simply bought me closer to God because sometimes, most of the time, He was all I had. In my world, I don't have to prove to ANYBODY that I am a Jew.

I think recent events have shown that misconduct and corruption exists in every organized religion, so it has become pointless to argue the superiority of one over the other.

As of right now, we are holding on to relics of our religious past. Jesus ain't gonna save us, but neither will Allah or Hashem; our spirituality will. Whatever it is that each of us believes in personally is what will save us; it is our Chayah that will save us, the very thing that personally connects us with our truth and our God.

Passover84—

Passover Seder 1984. I'm the little one with the fro down front.

Emunah and Iddo

1st Alayah—

The first time I was called to Torah.

My fifth grade class, twenty years ago.

Iddo's fifth grade class two years ago.

Women graduating from the academy
but not being awarded ordination.

My classmates and Rabbi. From left Mikhiel T., Yahath B., Tamar M.,
Rabbi Capers Funnye, Rabbi Joshua Salter, Mikhiel M.

21042243R00079

Made in the USA
Lexington, KY
02 March 2013